W9-DIM-037

GREAT LEADERS SEE THE FUTURE FIRST

*Taking Your Organization to the
Top in Five Revolutionary Steps*

Carolyn Corbin

DEARBORN™
A **Kaplan Professional** Company

This publication is designed to provide accurate and authoritative information in regard to the subject matter covered. It is sold with the understanding that the publisher is not engaged in rendering legal, accounting, or other professional service. If legal advice or other expert assistance is required, the services of a competent professional should be sought.

HD
57.7
.C67
2000

Senior Acquisitions Editor: Jean Iversen
Senior Managing Editor: Jack Kiburz
Interior Design: Lucy Jenkins
Cover Design: Design Solutions
Typesetting: Elizabeth Pitts

Published by Dearborn, a Kaplan Professional Company

Printed in the United States of America

00 01 02   10 9 8 7 6 5 4 3 2 1

Library of Congress Cataloging-in-Publication Data

Corbin, Carolyn, 1946–
    Great leaders see the future first : taking your organization to the top in five
revolutionary steps / Carolyn Corbin.
        p.   cm.
    Includes bibliographical references and index.
    ISBN 0-7931-3685-7 (6 × 9 hardcover)
    1. Leadership. 2. Executive ability. 3. Strategic planning. 4. Management.   I. Title.

HD57.7.C67   2000
658.4′092—dc21   00-022732

DEDICATION

Dedicated to my husband,

Ray Corbin,

already a great leader

OTHER BOOKS BY CAROLYN CORBIN

Strategies 2000

Conquering Corporate Codependence:
Lifeskills for Making It Within
or Without the Corporation

CONTENTS

STEP 2   Order the Chaos

STEP 3   Blend Multiple Organizational Models

ACKNOWLEDGMENTS

This book was written with the help and encouragement of many people. I offer special thanks to the following individuals who have supported me in the untold hours spent in preparing this work:

Sylvia Odenwald, who nurtured this project from the time it was a seed of thought to the moment it became a volume of work and who knew how to turn my dream into reality.

Carol Shockey, researcher, editor, and compiler, who gave enormous insight and framework to every page.

Euna Brady, Center for the 21st Century's director of administration, for encouragement, hard work, coordination, and friendship.

Summer Johnson, California graphic designer, for her unique ideas, dedication to the project, and the hard work that went into the graphics.

All those who granted interviews, gave generously of their time, and helped in untold ways: Lori Arguelles, David C. Balch, John A. Challenger, Richard Chang, Vance D. Coffman, Dr. Diana C. Dale, Ginger L. Ebinger, Marsha Johnson Evans, John C. Fryer Jr., Susan Germann, Harry Gossett, Frances Hesselbein, Andy Holdgate, Glenn R. Jones, Stephen Katsanos, Kay Kennedy, Bonnie Kirschenbaum, Dr. Jeffrey Lenn, Jim Mellado, Paul H. O'Neill, Nancy Ortberg, Tom Peddicord, Kurt Petersen, Valerie Pike, Jessica Poole, Peggy Pruett, Janice Reeb, Joyce Richards, Randy Robason, Fred Roberts, Henry Rogers, Dr. David W. Stewart, Art Stricklin, Gil A. Stricklin, Jim Stuart, Lynn Taylor, Megan Taylor, Peter B. Teets, Sharon Tennison, Senator George Voinovich, Tracy Zampaglione, Joy Zeigler, and Kelly Zitlow.

Members of the Christian Leadership Think Tank who provided spiritual input, challenged my ideas, examined my research, shared their spiritual wisdom, taught me patiently, and offered supportive prayers: Dr. Travis Berry, Euna Brady, Bette Huston, Scott Johnson, Jimmie Powell, Dr. James Puckett, Barbara L. Sleeper, and John Weber.

Cynthia Zigmund, associate publisher at Dearborn, for her faith in the project and guidance along the way.

Jean Iversen, senior acquisitions editor at Dearborn, for her dedicated interaction, enthusiasm, and encouragement from idea to reality.

Jack Kiburz, senior managing editor at Dearborn, for his excellent input, thorough editing, guidance, and patient answering of many questions.

Numerous friends and family members, who lovingly supported, encouraged, called, e-mailed, inquired, wrote, provided comic relief, and stood by until the end.

PREFACE

The World Needs Great Leaders

People are constantly searching for great leaders—those special individuals who have ethical character, care about their followers, and have the courage to lead them into a positive future. Yet there are few great leaders in existence today. The world is changing at lightning speed. Those who are good leaders today will not be good enough in the not-too-distant future. That's what this book is all about—becoming a great leader under a new set of global rules.

It is difficult to move into the future if you can't see where you're going. However, there are ways to monitor the future and view it with some clarity. For over 20 years, I have consulted with organizations to help them formulate their desired futures. I have worked with hundreds of companies and all levels of government as well as nonprofit organizations, educational and religious institutions, universities, and health care facilities. In all of these organizations, great leaders dare to envision the future. They then decide what to do about the future they see. They have the choice of accepting that future or trying to counter the direction in which things seem to be moving. Living life as a great leader takes an enormous amount of courage, wisdom, and expertise.

At times, it is difficult to see an accurate future. In the late 1960s, I was heavily involved in experimenting with computer-assisted instruction for public schools. In speeches and periodicals, I would claim that someday students could learn via self-paced instruction on their own computers. People actually laughed at the idea. Why? Because with the technology of the 1960s and early 1970s, it would have been unlikely that schools could afford computing capacity. At that time, mainframes had to be stored on raised floors in a very cool, temperature-controlled computer room. Those computers were huge. Terminals could be hooked to them, but, even so, computers in the classroom were highly unlikely. Then I dared say that computers would be in homes someday. Based on the same line of thinking, I was told that my ideas "just wouldn't work." Where the leaders failed in the 1960s was in the area of vision. All they could see were the mainframe models that existed at the time. They could not foresee the new technology that would make PCs possible and in turn change the course of history.

Organizations are recognizing the value in looking ahead. Scanning the horizon for various internal and external trends, global changes, economic booms and busts, and demographic peaks and valleys is part of the regular routine in many enterprises. Human resources professionals are becoming adept at taking on this responsibility. Currently, I serve as president of the Center for the 21st Century, a think tank I founded that is peopled with researchers who have surmised that the human resources arena soon will have an additional function: monitoring the organization's future to ensure positioning the enterprise for maximum impact.

This book has become more than an inspired idea. It has taken on a life of its own and has turned into a full-blown project. Researchers here at the Center for the 21st Century explored areas of interest through interviews and an extensive literature survey. By getting out in the field and actually experiencing the real world, we were able to form a more exact picture of the steps that good leaders must take to become great. *Great Leaders See the Future First* will guide you through these insights that we as a team have developed.

One thing we know for certain is that the world will change more rapidly than you have ever experienced. The recent past was merely a dress rehearsal for what is to come. My hope is that you will be as excited about the coming years as I am. You *can* have a tremendous impact. This book will tell you how.

—Carolyn Corbin
President, Center for the 21st Century

STEP 1

Orchestrate a 360° Worldview

CHAPTER 1

Taking Leadership to the Next Level

Leaders determine whether an organization succeeds or fails.

I have come to this conclusion after exploring workplace changes over the past 15 years and writing two other books on socioeconomic subjects. The first book, *Strategies 2000*, resulted from an IBM leader's astute assessment of the future. While I was on a consulting assignment with IBM, the leader approached me about conducting research and presenting a seminar to IBM employees about what would happen between 1985 and the year 2000. He told me that he perceived that as competition became stiffer, IBM would eventually be forced to do something that they had never done before—downsize significant numbers of people. He wanted the people in the group he managed to envision the future so they could plan ahead.

In conducting the research, I became so fascinated with the information that I used the original idea to conduct detailed research in 1986 that reached beyond the initial IBM assignment. From this research I formulated the observations that eventually became *Strategies 2000*, a book in which I made some bold claims. At the time, Japanese business was a real threat to U.S. manufacturers. Oil prices had dropped to approximately $9 per barrel. Hundreds of thousands of people were losing their jobs. The future seemed frightening. Yet in the book I claimed that by the year 2000, the United States would be experiencing prosperity. I also warned the workforce, including leaders, that it would be wise to become career self-reliant. I coined a word to describe this independent free agent who is capable of working within and without an organizational structure—*indipreneur*. The second book, *Conquering Corporate Codependence*, focused on the skills necessary to be a successful indipreneur.

Approximately 95 percent of the observations I made about the turn of the century in *Strategies 2000* are happening today—or have already happened. When the book first entered the marketplace, corporate executives kept a safe distance because they were afraid their employees might find the ideas unsettling. However, GE Credit Corporation grasped the philosophy and made *Strategies 2000* available to all employees, according to Harry Gossett, a former territory personnel and training manager. GE's chairman, Jack Welch, held a similar philosophy to that presented in *Strategies 2000*. Thus, GE Credit saw the value in asking its employees to become career self-reliant. The book's ideas began to spread. The observations that I made began to gain attention. Not only are those ideas prevalent today in business, but they are also expanding into nonprofit and government organizations as well.

Many people who read *Strategies 2000* in 1986 said that much of what I predicted could not possibly happen. Yet most of the forecasts have come to pass. Many people may feel that some of the claims in this present book may seem improbable. But I feel that a great percentage of the projections I make about the future will indeed happen.

As founder and president of the Center for the 21st Century, a think tank based in Dallas, Texas, I work with organizations of all types and sizes from the Fortune 500 to small entrepreneurial shops. My associates and I help organizational leaders formulate a vision of their organization's future and aid them in implementing plans to reach their long-term goals. The Center for the 21st Century assists leaders in defining and accomplishing their desired futures. We disseminate our information via keynote speeches, consulting, training sessions, executive briefings, books, articles in magazines and journals, and the Internet Web site <www.c21c.com>.

LEADERSHIP AT ALL LEVELS

At the Center for the 21st Century, we are noticing that leadership is increasingly required throughout the organization—not just at executive levels. The numbers of knowledge workers—workers who earn their living by analyzing, managing, and making judgments based on knowledge extracted from information—are growing exponentially. These types of workers will be called on to exhibit leadership skills at one time or another. Thus, in increasing numbers of cases, leaders are also considered to be workers. The line between leaders and workers is blurring. The only difference may lie in the type of work or function that each category performs. Throughout this book, leadership and management will be used synonymously. I feel strongly that managers must be leaders and that leaders must have at least a general knowledge of management techniques. In the 21st century, being good is not enough. Instead, leaders must operate at the next level—they must be great. Great leaders understand that they must see the future first, decide how to go there, and know what to do *before* they arrive.

I agree with Peter Drucker's observation that 90 percent of all organizations are led in similar ways.[1] Leadership is not confined solely to the large and small business domain but is equally important in government, nonprofits, religious organizations, health care, educational institutions, and in the family structure. In this work, I concentrate on the similarities of leaders in all organizations.

Many of today's leaders exist at a level on which they have been operating successfully for the past two decades. I call this Level 1. Rather than moving beyond Level 1, leaders are seeking to mature at the present level. The question is, Should leaders do more of the same better, or should they move to an advanced operating level? Leaders must learn to function at the next level, or Level 2. Continuing to exist on Level 1 will soon render a leader obsolete.

Beginning in the early 1970s, business became highly competitive. During the 1980s and 1990s, organizations were forced to streamline operations and reduce overhead to compensate for ever-decreasing profit margins. By the late 1990s, many organizations had become highly productive and were taking part in the American economic boom. As the calendar rolled over into the 21st century, organizations found themselves wanting to do even better. To maintain the high level of productivity in an even more competitive global marketplace, leaders must think and operate quite differently in the future.

To determine the level at which you are presently operating, please complete the following short exercise in Figure 1.1.

FIGURE 1.1   Leadership Level Evaluation Exercise

Instructions: The following questions should be answered either *yes* or *no*. They pertain to leadership roles in all types of organizations—large and small businesses, nonprofits, religious and educational institutions, and government organizations. Remember that *workers* may be either paid workers or volunteers.

1. Do you have a big-picture, ten-year plan for your organization?
2. Have you implemented technology to cut service processing time or product manufacturing turnaround time?
3. Are the people in your organization assigned work according to their personal values and work styles?
4. Do you have a core group of workers that are *permanent* with the remainder (up to 66 percent) of your workforce considered to be project workers?
5. Do you reevaluate your organization's methods for executing the organizational mission at least once per year?
6. Do you consider workers' relational skills as important as their technical skills?
7. Are techniques in place in your organization that allow you to access information on how other institutions or industries are responding to their marketplace/target areas?
8. Have you implemented a program to assess typical worker behaviors during change, and do you have a plan in place to preempt those behaviors that happen during the chaos stage of change?
9. Do you concentrate on developing new products, services, and ideas while trying to continuously improve those products and services that you now have in place?
10. Do you have a system presently operating that provides data on each worker's contribution to organizational goals?
11. Have you evaluated your organization and identified components of all systems? (Marketing, training, and knowledge management are some examples of organizational systems.)
12. Has your organization conducted a worker values analysis?
13. Does your organization have a method for constantly assessing trends and conducting issue analysis?
14. Have you implemented an atmosphere that is comfortable, motivational, and conducive to creativity and innovation?

FIGURE 1.1   Leadership Level Evaluation Exercise (cont.)

15. Do you hold meetings only when such alternative methods as conference calls, teleconferencing, or e-mail communication are not workable?

16. Have you implemented a system for telecommuting, hoteling, and other virtual office techniques for those workers who could be more productive in that environment?

17. Do you have a successful method for recruiting, retaining, and constantly training state-of-the-art workers?

18. Does your organization have an acceptable budget for research and development?

19. Are you constantly looking for ways to cut work process time in half?

20. Has your organization identified worker competencies and assigned work based on these competencies?

21. Are you using such cutting edge technology as e-commerce and Internet Web sites to communicate with and sell to your target customers?

22. Can you describe the business you are in by using no more than ten key words?

Scoring: For each *yes* answer give yourself 3 points. Higher scores indicate that you are leading at a higher level and are more prepared for the 21st century.

Total Points _____

Scoring Key

59–66 Congratulations! You are leading largely on the next level—Level 2—which will be a necessity by 2010.

46–58 You are a transitional leader with skills on both Level 1 and Level 2. By focusing on the areas you need to strengthen, you can move easily to Level 2, where you ultimately need to be.

0–45 You are largely a Level 1 leader and will be obsolete during the first decade of the 21st century. You need to focus on the steps for moving up to Level 2, which are covered in subsequent chapters.

Let's discuss Level 1 and Level 2 so you can determine what you need to do to move to the second level, unless your scores indicate that you are already operating on Level 2.

OPERATING AT LEVEL 1

Nine indicators reveal that leaders are operating at Level 1 when they do the following:

1. React to marketplace conditions
2. Favor hard skills
3. Are constantly busy
4. Lead in a fast operating mode
5. Concentrate on gathering and analyzing information
6. Manage turbulence
7. Employ traditional methods of marketing and communicating
8. Regard workers and organization as static and position oriented
9. Sacrifice innovation to pursue continuous improvement

React to Marketplace Conditions

Flexibility is at a premium, and leaders must move at warp speed so their organization's revenue will not be adversely affected. For example, the airline industry suffers from employee strikes. Leaders are caught reacting to severe customer inconveniences. The rapid introduction of e-commerce companies on the Internet is causing traditional companies to scramble to create e-commerce departments solely for the purpose of offering their products and services for sale on the Internet. Not being on the Internet can be devastating to an organization. Because many institutions never anticipated the impact of the Internet, they are forced into a reactionary mode.

Favor Hard Skills

During the industrial revolution, bottom-line hard numbers began to drive corporations. In most cases, the bottom line continues to be the primary measurement of an organization's success. Being able to measure the bottom-line numbers is important—extremely important. However, are hard numbers always the endgame in determining organizational success? Are membership numbers entirely indicative of a church's achievement? Are profits the sole determinant of a corporation's attainment? Change agents who approach organizational transition in a mechanistic way are hitting a brick wall. For example, downsizing that results in overworking the survivors is demoralizing. Commitment is lost. Mistrust prevails. The price for efficiency is being paid with the cost of effectiveness.

Are Constantly Busy

Many leaders, especially those in a nonbusiness entity, are content to remain busy. But busy does not always mean productive. As change happens rapidly, organizations find themselves stricken by analysis paralysis, and leaders of these organizations feel that being busy justifies their existence.

I was recently called into a nonprofit organization to assess its operating environment and recommend ways to increase productivity. I refer to the organization as the CE Corporation, although that is not its real name. I immediately observed the seemingly incessant meetings that the leaders were attending. Every time I met executives in the hallway, they were charging forward to attend yet another meeting. The senior managers were always tired and seemingly overworked. They constantly complained about not having enough hours in the workday.

Then I attended one of CE Corporation's all-day meetings and discovered a major problem. The president ran the meeting on an unfocused, loose agenda with a lot of debate but without reaching consensus. The meeting was adjourned only to set a time for another session to rehash the last meeting. Busy, yes! Productive, absolutely not! Valuable time, energy, and money were being wasted.

Lead in a Fast Operating Mode

The organizational environment today is fast. Change happens so rapidly that executives must run just to keep up with the status quo. In fact, a very successful business magazine is appropriately entitled *Fast Company*.[2] Shortly, however, the current speed defining *fast* will not be fast enough. The economic climate is such that organizations are experiencing tremendous prosperity. What will happen when global competition increases? Is the present level of speed adequate?

Concentrate on Gathering and Analyzing Information

One of the hallmarks of a leader is to make good, quick decisions based on adequate information. The present level of information gathering for decision making is rapidly becoming obsolete. It is not enough to identify mission, assess strengths and weaknesses, identify target markets, know the competition, and formulate a rather short-term, stop-gap game plan based solely on knowledge and information gleaned from an isolated executive team. Successful decision making requires more.

Manage Turbulence

For the past two decades, leaders have been asked to manage their organization in the midst of turmoil. It is now a given assumption that organizations are complex systems and that chaos will abound a majority of the time. Leaders assume the only thing that can be done with chaos is to live in it and manage it to the best of their ability. Even mathematicians believe that most chaos is unpredictable, thus catapulting the people leading these organizations into an eternal reactionary mode.

Employ Traditional Methods of Marketing and Communicating

Surprisingly, I continue to see organizations trying to reach their customers in the same ways they have used for several years. They employ media advertising, direct mail, and telephone solicitation without considering electronic online media. Many suppliers continue to sell strictly through retail walk-in establishments. Religious and educational institutions invest heavily in facilities that indicate the institutions' assumption that their customers will continue to come to them as in the past. They proliferate the *talking head* approach. Lengthy newsletters doubling as marketing tools arrive in the mail, only to be glanced at and thrown away.

Approaching the arenas of marketing and communicating as they have always done is causing many organizations to miss innovative and lucrative opportunities.

Regard Workers and Organization as Static and Position Oriented

Other than rightsizings and natural attrition, companies have assumed that the people in organizations are relatively static. There continues to be an unwritten understanding that the majority of employees are hired to be permanent and occupy a specific position within the organizational structure.

One major corporate executive has commented to me that he hopes the relationship with everyone he hires will be permanent. "Like a marriage," he indicated, "not all employer-employee relationships work out. Our organization hires workers. If our needs change, we downsize. It's less expensive to have permanent workers on our payroll than to work with great numbers of temporary labor in order to avert layoffs."

I question that philosophy. I also question that it is less expensive—all compensation and other costs considered—to hire permanent employees rather than outsource certain work or contract project workers.

Sacrifice Innovation to Pursue Continuous Improvement

Although change seems to be constant, leaders feel that one of their major goals is to do what they are now doing even better. Continuous improvement is understood to be an avenue to progress and greater quality of customer satisfaction. Although constantly refreshing present products and services is commendable, it is not enough. Customers bore easily. The competition will be introducing newer products and services. By concentrating solely on continuous improvement of existing products and services, organizations will eventually render themselves obsolete.

The nine characteristics discussed above describe leadership on today's level—Level 1. To rise to the challenges of the near future, however, leaders must move up to Level 2, the level of great leadership during the first decade of the 21st century.

MOVING TO LEVEL 2

By the year 2010, great leaders must be on Level 2 or they will be ineffective. When leaders climb from Level 1 to Level 2, they will make nine transitional movements:

Level 1	Level 2
1. Reacting	1. Strategizing
2. Emphasizing hard skills	2. Focusing on the whole person
3. Being busy	3. Becoming productive
4. Leading in a fast environment	4. Leading at warp speed
5. Gathering information	5. Gathering intelligence
6. Managing turbulence	6. Preempting chaos
7. Employing traditional methods	7. Operating via electronic mode
8. Managing positions	8. Managing people flow
9. Doing the same things better	9. Improving processes through innovative ideas, products, and services

Strategizing

Instead of merely being flexible and reacting to rapid change, great leaders will adapt and use proactive strategy. A new form of strategic planning is emerging that involves a ten-year, big-picture, flexible plan. Even though the future seems to be a moving target, it is necessary to plan for it. Although strategic planning has been around for a long time, two new pieces have been added. The first piece involves projecting things that might occur and mustering the resources necessary for such contingencies. In the past, planners would strategize what *will be*. Now they must strategize what *might be*, assess the probability of occurrence, and be ready for each event that is highly probable.

Another piece of today's strategic plan is that it is now formulated by the whole company and no longer just by the leaders. Often, workers see trends and sense necessary competitive moves before executives detect them. Although strategic thinking can be taught, some workers are more naturally gifted in that area. Identifying those people and honing their specific skills adds to organizational effectiveness.

Focusing on the Whole Person

Hard skills are not all there is to organizational success. More than ever before, soft skills help to determine an entity's destiny. A person comes to work, lives in a community, may volunteer at a local charity, and may have a particular religious affiliation. The quality of home life affects all other aspects of a person's existence. Conversely, the quality of all other aspects of one's reality affects the individual's home life.

Traditional male domains are slowly feminizing. Women generally offer such soft skills as nurturing, emotional intelligence, and relationship cultivation. As more women have joined the workforce, typically hard masculine skills of bottom-line orientation and numeric measurement are being combined with traditionally soft feminine skills to form an androgynous organization—a place that addresses the needs of the whole person.

Becoming Productive

Being busy is no longer enough. Becoming measurably productive is important. The measurement of productivity requires that an organization have a strategy stating what the organization has set out to achieve. In a given period, actual achievements are measured against mutually agreed-on targets. In the industrial world, productivity can be defined as output-per-person-hour. In the arena of the knowledge worker, productivity is defined differently. Successful outcomes within a specific period most nearly equate to knowledge worker productivity. Both quantity and quality must be taken into consideration. The end user's feedback is also very important in rating productivity in this information age.

Because time is a key variable in the productivity equation, nonessential busy tasks must be eliminated. The idea is to accomplish as much as possible within budget and time constraints while pleasing the end user.

Leading at Warp Speed

Fast will become faster. As Europe, Asia, and more third-world countries become greater contenders in the global economy, the speed with which products and services will be introduced into the marketplace will increase. Stiffer competition will breed the need for faster transactions and more innovation. Rapid reaction to marketplace change is not enough. Executives must think at the rate of warp speed.

Warp speed is redefining the whole global power and economic structure. This revolutionary, earthquakelike shift is rumbling through every organization. The message is *keep up or step aside*. Those people who can lead the organization at this unprecedented rate of speed will be compensated well—both monetarily and psychologically.

For this to happen, great leaders must be totally committed to the organization's mission. A major challenge will be workers' stress tolerance. At some point, pressure becomes so great that morale and commitment break down. To avert this disaster, workers will be forced, through self-defense, to find creative ways to cope. Work must be structured to balance the stress load. Teamwork must be promoted. The work environment must be designed for stress reduction.

Gathering Intelligence

Decision making based on random single source data gathered by subordinates or independent agencies falls short of expectations of dynamic leadership. Leaders will drive the intelligence gathering that takes place in their organization.

Whole units will be responsible for gathering, housing, analyzing, synthesizing, reporting, and managing information to convert it into practical, useful knowledge. This systematic process of converting information to knowledge is known as gathering intelligence—or intelligence gathering. Knowledge workers will specialize in specific areas of intelligence gathering. For example, competitive intelligence, which is knowledge about the organization's competitive market, has become so popular that an association—the Society of Competitive Intelligence Professionals—caters to people engaged in the field.

Preempting Chaos

Because turmoil is destructive, leaders will learn to preempt chaos rather than manage in spite of it. Knowing that chaos is a predictable phase of change, leaders can learn ways to reduce the consequences of the transition process. By anticipating factors that might arise, great leaders introduce interventions as preemptive strikes against organizational turbulence. Survivors of chaos are always different after the period of turmoil than they were before the turbulence was introduced. If the chaos is severe, the people in power before the turmoil in many cases are not the same people who rise to prominence in the renewed organization. The classic illustration of this concept is the demise of the big, powerful dinosaur after a sudden shift in the planetary environment. The mammal became the dominant species when the dinosaur could no longer survive.

Operating via Electronic Mode

Online organizational business is moving forward much faster than most leaders expected. I call the transition a movement from *t-mode* to *e-mode*, or traditional to electronic mode. Retailing will never be the same again. Buying and selling by electronic means will replace much of the traditional walk-in, phone-in, and mail-order business. Stocks and bonds, books, banking services, automobiles, travel, toys, and toothpaste—all can be bought through the Internet.

Almost everything possible is being distributed online. The middleperson is becoming extinct. This phenomenon of combining business with technology has become so universal that it now has a name—e-business or e-commerce—and universities are scrambling to offer degrees in the new discipline.

The letter *e* for electronic will precede, and already is preceding, many industry categories; for example, e-publishing, e-tailing, and e-medicine. The Internet will become the number-one medium for organizational business-to-business transactions.

Consumer spending online is at least doubling each year, a phenomenon that equates and even exceeds the initial growth of the telephone, automobile, or television. Great leaders must grasp this organizational medium or face extinction. Obviously, dot.com companies generate most, if not all, of their business online. Such large companies as IBM, Ford, and General Motors could have 25 to 50 percent of revenue generated through e-commerce by 2005.

Managing People Flow

With stiff competition and reduced profit margins staring all organizations in the face, great leaders will become adept at managing people flow. No longer will organizations consider a majority of their employees as permanent. In the estimation of the Center for the 21st Century, between 2015 and 2025, at least 70 percent of the workforce will be nonpermanent. The organization will allocate most workers to projects, keeping them only for the duration of a project and then moving them to other projects or releasing them from the organization. The management of this flux of people will be an important skill.

Professionals will establish specialized careers in allocating people to projects and then swiftly moving them onward or outward. Organizations of the future will not be able to keep people on the payroll if workers' time is not directly chargeable to a revenue-producing source or if their time has not been prebudgeted, as in the case of knowledge workers who are conducting research and development.

This flux of workers will breed what I call an *elastic employee*—a worker capable of moving within an organization or from organization to organization on project work. When specialists are recruiting such workers, they will look for distinct qualities of independence coupled with an ability to work on ad hoc teams. This special breed of worker will thrive on self-governance and excel at cooperative relational skills. Recruiters don't search for persons seeking long-term work in the organization but merely those who want a contractual commitment to the immediate project.

Improving Processes through Innovative Ideas, Products, and Services

Innovation will be as important as continuous improvement. Innovators will win the competition game in the future. To rival your competition or even *become* the competition, it will be necessary to revolutionize your industry. Timing is everything. Innovations must be introduced simultaneously with consumer acceptance. If the timing is off for either introduction of the innovation or consumer acceptance, the mission will fail. Such timing requires detailed intelligence gathering, accurate vision, and precise market timing.

The world of innovation is no place for faint-of-heart leaders. The stakes are high. The game is risky. Only the best will survive. Yet without innovation, strategy, and execution, no organization will last in the vicious marketplace.

Among other necessary skills, workers must be recruited for their creative-thinking abilities. Training programs and work itself will require creativity of everyone involved. Doing the same things the same way for three years or more will eventually kill an organization.

FIVE GIANT STEPS TO BECOMING A GREAT LEADER

Very few leaders today are operating totally on Level 2. However, it is possible to step up to Level 2 quickly by taking five giant steps:

1. Orchestrate a 360° worldview.
2. Order the chaos.
3. Blend multiple organizational models.
4. Engage the whole person.
5. Ignite innovation.

In the remainder of the book, each of these steps is discussed.

How to Use the Leadership Strategies and Questions for Contemplation in This Book

At the end of each chapter are two sections: Leadership Strategies and Questions for Contemplation. Although many tactics are discussed in the chapter text, the Leadership Strategies section offers suggestions for implementing some of the principles discussed throughout the chapter.

In the Questions for Contemplation section, I list questions aimed at promoting creative and critical thinking and that are most useful when used in a think tank setting. In forming a think tank, call together a group of people from different disciplines to gather a broad view of an issue. The disciplines involved will depend on the issues at hand. These members should be from within your organization or from other organizations and/or interest groups to ensure a broader perspective. The most innovative ideas often come from outside your organization—even outside your industry.

Meet on a regular basis for a specific amount of time (one to four hours) to address issues and provide suggestions for the solution of problems. As the group blends various points of view from differing areas of expertise, interesting results will emerge. After the purpose has been achieved, the same group can either disband or become involved in implementing solutions.

One suggestion might be to take a chapter per week over an 11-week period and hold a think tank session for each chapter. Only your imagination can limit ways to use the Questions for Contemplation.

 # LEADERSHIP STRATEGIES

The major thrust in this chapter has been to emphasize the necessity for leaders to move from a Level 1 mode of operation to Level 2. These are the steps to accomplish this move:

✓ Identify each area in which you exist on Level 1.

✓ Determine the steps you need to take to move to Level 2.

✓ Set a goal to be totally on Level 2 within one year. Failure to operate at Level 2 will hurt a leader's career in the next decade.

QUESTIONS FOR CONTEMPLATION

1. Which questions in the Leadership Level Evaluation Exercise were answered with *no?*

2. What immediate steps can you take to change the *no* answers to *yes* answers within one year?

3. Does your organization have a strategic plan?

4. If yes, is it being implemented?

5. If not, what initiatives must be taken to develop one?

6. Is the speed of processes changing in your organization?

7. What factors are driving the change?

8. What steps has your organization taken to reduce worker stress under rapid change?

9. What sources do you use to gather intelligence?

10. What do you need to do to improve your intelligence-gathering system?

11. Have you identified the need to measure people flow in your organization?

12. If not, do you need to implement processes to accomplish this measurement?

ENDNOTES

1. Peter Drucker, "Management's New Paradigms," *Forbes*, 5 October 1998, 156.
2. Alan M. Webber, "Learning for a Change," *Fast Company*, May 1999, 178–188.

CHAPTER 2

Gathering Organizational Intelligence

Growing more restless after sitting on the runway for more than two hours, I thought, Is this plane ever going to take off? The pilot interrupted my musing with this message, "Ladies and gentlemen, we are going back to the gate to deplane. Our right wing compass is out of order, and in aviation terminology, that is a *no go* situation." Without direction-finding instruments, the pilot couldn't navigate. Of course, there were the normal mumbles and grumbles, but I think we were all secretly happy that the problem had been detected. The bad news was that we would be late to our destination. The good news was that we had a better chance of reaching it on another plane.

The above episode provides an example of organizations that will not meet competitive challenges in the future. The idea is simple: Some organizations have visionary leadership and some do not. Those who do will be the *go* organizations five years from now. Those who do not will be the *no go* enterprises of the future. The organizational leader, who should be the foremost direction finder, must be the visionary. In reviewing the characteristics of great leaders, I find a striking commonality. They all have a relatively clear view of the future. Great leaders see the future first and develop their plans for survival and success around their vision. Some of them see the writing on the wall and devise plans to take full advantage of ensuing circumstances. Others create their own opportunities. And in so doing, they create their future.

Take Bill Gates, for example. His vision of a dominant operating system in personal computers (PCs) has revolutionized the world. Abraham Lincoln pictured a nation without slavery and worked to realize that vision. The late President John F. Kennedy envisioned a person walking on the moon before the 1960s came to an end. Jeff Bezos anticipated the tremendous potential of e-commerce and founded Amazon.com. The great civil rights leader Martin Luther King, Jr. saw a nation where people related to one another by what was on the inside—not by skin color.

Lockheed Martin's former Chairman and CEO Norman R. Augustine states that Lockheed Martin remained successful during a time when markets for the defense industry had shrunk by more than 50 percent because the company's leaders had the wisdom to "read the tea leaves."[1] Current Chairman and CEO Vance D. Coffman exemplifies this by saying, "In truth, the factory of tomorrow can be found between our employees' ears today."[2]

Although it is not a new skill, the ability to have a clear vision of tomorrow is rapidly becoming a cornerstone of leadership. Tomorrow's explosive opportunities are hinted at today. Those leaders keen enough to perceive the clues have a prime window of opportunity to pilot their organization into a very successful future.

Many people would claim that visioning is a game for mystics and crystal ball gazers. However, we at the Center for the 21st Century believe that observing the future is a leadership skill—both an art and a science involving astute reasoning, observational acumen, and connection skills derived from qualitative and quantitative methodologies. In Chapter 1, I defined this systematic process of converting information to useful targeted knowledge as *intelligence gathering*.

THE BUSINESS OF INTELLIGENCE GATHERING

Governments and the military have long been engaged in intelligence work. In many cases during the Cold War, intelligence gathering moved beyond ethical boundaries and became espionage. Hollywood producers dramatized espionage in feature films and introduced advanced and exciting technology for use by the hero to bring the plot to a satisfactory conclusion. Most of us have probably gripped the arms of our movie seats as an intriguing spy mystery unfolded. However, many of those scenes may be closer to truth than to fiction as more sophisticated technology is introduced.

Although nations continue to be in the intelligence business, intelligence gathering has also spread into the business arena. In spite of the fact that unethical intelligence practices do result in corporate espionage, I am talking here about the legal and ethical conversion of information into purposeful knowledge to help a business organization compete. Intelligence can be gathered for all sorts of reasons—improving customer services, detecting the competition's new products and services, determining the technology needed to increase productivity, and perhaps assembling a database for housing internal intelligence. The list goes on and on.

As global competition heats up in the first decade of the 21st century, business intelligence could become a $100 billion industry. New careers will be created to handle the burgeoning field. The first major challenge of intelligence gathering is where to find the dependable data you need. The second major challenge is acquiring the skills necessary to make expedient use of this information. Powerful decisions are made based on the intelligence at hand. Just as accomplished pilots must have the ability to read their instruments accurately when sight is impossible, great leaders must make critical decisions based on intelligence when it is impossible to create a vision any other way.

In this chapter we will introduce a model for creating your organizational vision and seven areas where intelligence can be gathered continually. This will increase the accuracy of your perception and give you a basis for your decisions.

A 360° WORLDVIEW

In the arctic regions of the world, an old tradition for hunters is to make blankets from animal hides and use them as a makeshift trampoline. The blanket is spread onto the ground, and one of the hunters stands on it. Several other hunters grasp the edges, heave the blanket upward, and eject the hunter high into the air to see if any caribou are in the area. The organizational leader must have similar skills. Though not physically thrown into the heavens, the leader must choose to rise above everyday events to view a snapshot of the future from above and get a 360° worldview.

The perspective of the future is divided into three segments—near future, future, and distant future. The near future is from now to 5 years hence, the future is from 5 to 10 years hence, and the distant future may be from 10 to 25 years away. Obviously, the near future is easier to see. If one looks closely enough, one can see the beginning of trends at least 5 years before they become common knowledge. The secret to winning in the competitive marketplace is being at the right place *before* the right time and then knowing how to take advantage of the information at hand.

TRENDS, CONDITIONS, AND ISSUES

Three terms are necessary for understanding a 360° worldview. Please consult Figure 2.1 as you read explanations of these terms.

The first term, *trend,* is a general direction. The second term, *condition,* is when multiple trends come together somewhere in the future. *Issue,* the third term, is an outcome and can be a conflict point when conditions emerge.

Let's take an example. In Texas, spring weather can be quite violent. I often become uneasy when I notice the sky becoming dark, the barometer dropping rapidly, the humidity going up, and the wind becoming still. When these trends come together in just the right combination, they may produce a condition known as a disastrous tornado, with severe damage occurring in seconds. In Texas we have a healthy respect for tornadoes and take precautions when we feel tornadic conditions might occur. If we do have tornado damage, several issues must be dealt with. For example, if I incur property damage, I need to telephone the insurance company, perhaps locate a place to stay while the damage is repaired, buy new furniture to replace the damaged lot, and try to control my stress level. Some of these issues can be points of conflict: The insurance may not pay all that I had hoped; there may be no hotel rooms left in town; my anxiety level may rise to new heights; and I may need medical attention.

Any person who has had experience with tornadoes knows to anticipate the conditions and issues that could arise and prepare in advance. When storm signals begin to fall into place, a window of opportunity to minimize the damage does exist. Individuals can seek

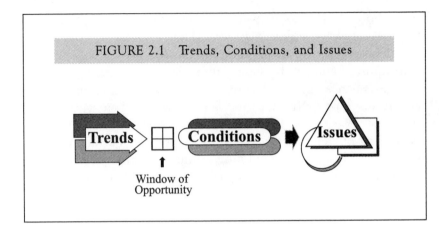

FIGURE 2.1   Trends, Conditions, and Issues

shelter, and some property, including automobiles, can be secured. Although damage may still occur, people can do their best to anticipate conditions and take proper actions. A wise person will at least have a good insurance program in place.

The same principles exist in the organization. A good leader is always on the lookout for emerging trends and tries to project ensuing conditions and issues. Just as an airline pilot must spend many hours in the flight simulator reviewing hypothetical situations, an organization's leadership must spend many hours creating scenarios relating to the future and anticipating the possibilities. Leaders picture the window of opportunity and take appropriate action. By creating pictorial images of the future, great leaders are often able to know what seems unknowable and act *before* a condition emerges.

Through our work at the Center for the 21st Century, we have discovered that organizations can prosper when they anticipate trends up to 5 years in advance and take appropriate action. Further, if people choose not to counter trends or trends are impossible to counter, they will become part of the culture and may even appear in a standard dictionary within 10 to 14 years.

In the late 1980s, Korn/Ferry International and Columbia University Graduate School of Business, in a joint study, asked 1,500 top executives in 20 countries their perspective on global marketing. Many leaders in the United States felt that domestic markets could support their businesses without the need to enter worldwide markets. Executives from other areas of the world felt that their prosperity hinged on going global.[3] However, as time passed and markets did indeed become global, the executives in the United States got busy, caught up, and surpassed many companies from other countries. One would wonder how far ahead the United States would be today had leaders recognized globalization earlier. Today, globalization is a given and is considered a part of the mainstream institutional culture.

WINDOW OF OPPORTUNITY

Between every set of trends and its ensuing conditions is a window of opportunity. Astute leaders understand that people with wisdom anticipate and intervene while human nature waits and reacts. Great leaders exercise wisdom rather than default to human nature.

Let's look at an example from local government. There may be early signs of racial unrest in a city or disagreement about specific issues. Different ethnic groups may disagree over city government policies. Leaders of different groups may appear, and street wars could break out from time to time. For the past two to five years, certain groups may have been asserting that local government officials are ignoring them. While these conditions continue, one of the scenarios that city officials might anticipate would be a riot—a condition based on overt trends.

However, in the early days of observing potentially dangerous trends, civic leaders could find the window of opportunity. Discussion could be started among different groups to find where the seed of agitation lies. Negotiations for improvement in policies for all the groups could take place. Leaders could hold diversity training for all groups; it is important to consider all issues that are causing conflict and discuss them openly. Make an effort to resolve conflicts before acts of terrorism occur or civil war breaks out. Wise leaders see the warning signals and open the window of opportunity for positive results. When the window of opportunity is ignored, results may be calamitous. In many cases, leaders ignore the window of opportunity in the hope that the trends will go away. Normally, however, trends escalate. Rarely do the danger signals disappear. Wise leaders never operate in ignorance but face potential problems head-on and seek solutions.

Four Ways to Address the Window of Opportunity

Denial. Some people suffer from the ostrich syndrome. They bury their heads in the sand, deny the existence of the circumstances they observe, and ignore the danger signals. For instance, an executive of a small nonprofit organization began to notice a lot of turnover among employees. Performance was low and funds were not being raised as they had been in the past, so he decided to conduct an employee attitude survey. The results showed that the employees were unhappy with *him*. They felt that he was not supportive, did not share enough of the workload, and was using organizational time for his own personal needs. Instead of using this information to improve his efforts, he became angry and blamed the employees for plotting against him. As a result, the organization faltered and began having great financial difficulty. His denial of the root of the problem cost the organization a competitive edge that it never regained.

Ignorance. Often, trends present themselves but leaders don't see them and are ignorant of their existence. Good observational skills require that people listen with both eyes and ears. Ironically, one of the reasons that leaders miss trends is "success arrogance." The organization seems to be doing so well that executives fail to see the danger signals. Some mainframe computer manufacturers, for example, were so successful that they failed to see the potential in the PC market and continued to manufacture mainframes while the competition was moving to smaller units. Arrogance can produce ignorance. What we know (or think we know) determines what we see. What we see determines our destination.

Arrogance is not the only reason we don't see trends. Not knowing how to look for them, or simply missing them, is also a factor. Even today in the educational arena, some universities don't see the need to become involved in virtual learning. The administration feels that education will take place in the future just as it has in the past. Wrong assumption! Those leaders with that attitude will be left behind—and so will the university.

Purposeful intervention. A great leader notices that consumers are increasingly using the Internet. With heavy time demands, consumers want to do business around the clock—any time, any place. Astute leaders notice that consumers are shopping differently and determine the feasibility of e-commerce on the Internet. By purposefully intervening and changing the direction of an organization's customer service and product sales, leaders successfully take the company into the future.

One of my nonprofit clients is experiencing unprecedented growth. Funds are being raised faster than the executive director can disperse them. For most nonprofit groups, this would be a dream come true. However, for this organization, growth is frustrating. It seems that there is not enough time to address donor needs. The office staff is improperly trained. The board is in conflict. Had the leaders of this organization created scenarios of success during the window of opportunity and practiced purposeful intervention, the chaos would not be so annoying.

Some people ask, "What about acts of God? Maybe the condition is out of our control—like a weather condition." The answer, "Practice the best purposeful interventions as are possible under the circumstances." For instance, the Oklahoma City tornadoes in May 1999 were some of the most devastating storms of the 20th century. No human intervention could have prevented these tornadoes. However, the weather service's early warning signals were heard by virtually everyone in the storm's path and people took shelter. Although some people lost their lives or were seriously injured, many lives were saved because people heeded the warnings and took advantage of the window of opportunity between the time that the storm siren blew and the tornado hit.

Acceptance. If all trends seem favorable, great leaders choose to accept the circumstances and enjoy the conditions as they happen.

A nonprofit organization that I work with is experiencing unprecedented prosperity. It is located in a booming suburban community that has increasing wealth seeded by the high-tech industry. The organization's cause is strong, and money is rolling in every day. The board of trustees and staff of this organization are enjoying the benefits of this robust economy and working hard to be good stewards of the donors' funds.

SEVEN MAJOR TRENDS AFFECTING THE WORLD

From a 360° worldview, there are seven major global trends that are changing how we live and work. These trends are culminating in four tidal wavelike conditions that will greatly impact our lives in unprecedented ways. Those leaders who understand the impact of these trends and take advantage of the window of opportunity to find points of success will reap untold rewards in the first quarter of the 21st century. The potential to discover life in real ways has never been better. Not only do we have tremendous possibilities for material gain, but emerging trends show us that we can climb to heights of spiritual fulfillment and quality. Never in the history of the world have we been at such an exciting point. Astute leaders will observe these trends, then decide how these inclinations will directly affect their organization. So many people spend time generating ideas about the future, but they fail to put plans into action. Prognostication is not enough. Intervention by design must take place.

In some of the Center for the 21st Century's small business client organizations, the leaders have formed think tanks that have been meeting for two years but have yet to design and implement an intervention. The members are having a great time brainstorming—or just being busy—but are not putting actions to their ideas and being productive. What a waste of the organization's time!

In surveying the seven global trends, I have gathered certain information that only skims the surface compared with the information you must gather about each trend to assess its impact on your particular organization.

1. Increasing Freedom

A man from East Germany walked up to me and placed in my hand a piece of the Berlin Wall. What a poignant moment! It was just a small sliver of shattered stone, but the significance was awesome. That portion of rock had fallen to the ground and the man had picked it up as the Berlin Wall was torn down in 1989. No longer were East and West Germany divided. Many people in East Germany were beginning to experience freedom for the first time in their life.

With the fall of the former Soviet Union, a new form of government introduced freedom to people who had never before felt independence. Confusion and chaos often accompany freedom because people who have never been free have no idea how to act when the walls of dependency are torn away. The former USSR is experiencing this chaos even after several years of freedom.

Simultaneously, in the United States there are increasing challenges to the Constitution's First Amendment freedoms. Questions arise: How much freedom do people in America have? Where does my freedom end and yours begin?

It appears that Americans are moving from *freedom from* to *freedom to*. America was founded on freedom from persecution or forced beliefs by the state. Now the country is moving far beyond those tenets to pushing freedom to its limits. The boundaries between freedom from and freedom to are growing thin.

Throughout the world people are experiencing increased freedom. As information reaches the uttermost parts of the globe, people are seeing and hearing about freedom. Those who yearn to be free are rebelling against persecution by totalitarian governments and exerting the energy to become free. The impetus for freedom and democracy is escalating.

This trend is also seen in the workplace. Employers are empowering their employees and independent contractors to exercise more decision-making freedom. When workers are freed from hierarchical controls, they must possess a different set of skills to be successful in the empowered organization. Many of the same skills that are necessary for organizational empowerment are needed for living in a civil democracy. Strangely enough, only a small percentage of workers possess these skills naturally—as small as 10 percent. The others must learn the skills for self-governance.

2. Increased Speed of Transportation

Imagine a hyperplane that can fly three to five times the speed of the Concorde! Traveling around the world will be simple. Making trips between continents will be fast. A globe-trotter can leave the United States in the morning for a meeting in London, attend the meeting, then fly back to the United States that evening in time for a late dinner with his family. The ironic twist to this scenario is that about the time we have very swift transportation, fewer trips will be needed. Technological interconnectivity will allow most business to be conducted without the participants having to be physically present. However, there will still be a need for fast transportation. And there will be vast numbers of people to take advantage of it.

3. Progressive World Peace

Although explosive terrorist attacks and civil wars seem on the increase in the world, world peace actually is progressing. For the first time in decades, the global superpowers are at peace with one another. Because of economic interdependence, a lot is at stake. Going to war with one of the superpowers would penalize a country's financial position.

The major fear today is not of war among the superpowers but of acts of terrorism by special interest groups and countries that possess nuclear weapons. Many of these acts will take place in the terrorist's native land. A jury has convicted a U.S. citizen for perpetrating one of the most heinous terrorist acts in the United States, the Oklahoma City bombing. School shootings reflect acts of terrorism by young Americans. Smaller countries committing acts of global terrorism are not superpowers. In the future, however, they will possess the power to destroy the world through nuclear weapons or biological warfare.

Progressive world peace means that more countries can enter the competitive financial arena. As third-world countries improve their lot and the people become more educated, their products and services will also be in the marketplace. Military competition is giving way to marketplace competition. Great leaders are prepared to vie for their place in the global financial arena.

4. Advancing Technology

Futurists tell us that the amount of information we have today will be 1 percent of the information available by the year 2050. Since the mid-1990s we have witnessed tremendous advances in the Internet and intranets within organizations. Technology is being miniaturized and appearing in new combinations. Telephones, television, and computers operating as one unit will eventually be in almost every household. The Internet has revolutionized the world. Many people believe that this is all there is to the information superhighway. However, Bill Gates indicates in his book *The Road Ahead* that the true information superhighway probably will not be available until at least 2005. Much hard work is left to do.[4]

With the exponential growth in technology throughout the world, the amount of information available and the complex skills that will be necessary to convert available information into practical knowledge will change dramatically.

5. Changing Capitalism

The United States has exercised capitalism in a semipure state since the 1930s. According to Lester Thurow, capitalism failed in the 1930s, so the United States was forced to add a socialistic element.[5] As countries become more competitive and adopt a capitalistic approach, capitalism will move toward a purer state excluding the socialistic element. This means that our government and others as well will be less supportive of such ideas as welfare and subsidies. These programs will either be totally eliminated or become the domain of volunteer organizations and religious institutions.

6. Increasing World Business Trade

With increasing freedom and speed of transportation, progressive superpower peace, advancing technology, and a purer state of capitalism, great increases in world business trade can be expected. Trade is increasingly important to the prosperity of the United States. According to the U.S. Department of Commerce, Bureau of Economic Analysis, the United States has an increasing trade surplus in services and an increasing trade deficit in goods.[6] Japan, China, Indonesia, India, and many other countries will continue emerging in world trade activities. Services and products will be traded throughout the world.

7. Increasing Understanding of Diversity

To open trade barriers, leaders must increase their understanding of diversity. The United States is becoming such a mosaic of minorities that no one group will be a majority by 2050. Only through understanding differences and working to unify citizens at a level surmounting our differences will we be able to relate peacefully in this changing environment. The U.S. paradigm of diversity will be modeled worldwide as the planet shrinks to a global community.

No organization can escape the need to view diversity as a positive influence on its success. The more we learn to live and work together, the more prosperous the world will be.

DYNAFORCES

The seven primary trends discussed above eventually interact to produce four major organization-changing conditions that I call DynaForces because they are dynamic forces full of energy and motion. These four DynaForces are *globalization, marketization, informatization,* and *democratization.* In order to influence the organization's future, smart leaders study the cross-impact of all trends and conditions and take advantage of the offered window of opportunity.

The next chapter takes a detailed look at these DynaForces.

 ## LEADERSHIP STRATEGIES

The strategies below emphasize the gathering of credible intelligence to help you, the leader, steer your organization into a desirable future.

✓ To gather valid intelligence, identify and locate dependable information sources that you can access repeatedly to monitor emerging trends and conditions. These sources might include trade journals, popular magazines, newspapers, online databases, newsletters, books, professional researchers, corporate executives in your field of interest, information brokers, accountants, physicians, consultants, attorneys, and economists. Set up a schedule for accessing your intelligence sources so that you can calculate variances in trends. Then follow the schedule you have set up.

✓ Continually be on the alert for new intelligence resources and make use of them.

✓ Practice making decisions based on the intelligence you have gathered. Keep records on the results of your decisions to determine the reliability of your resources.

✓ Create at least three scenarios about your organization's future. Monitor them at least once per quarter to see which scenario plays out. Be ready to implement your plans quickly.

✓ Constantly watch for trends approaching within the next five years. Look for recurrences such as two or three lawsuits in the same category that might escalate. Be prepared to handle these situations when they occur.

✓ Among other scenarios, create storyboards that play out organizational success. Plan your organizational resources that must be in place for the enterprise to expand. Be willing to take calculated risks to grow and prosper.

QUESTIONS FOR CONTEMPLATION

1. Do you have intelligence-gathering systems in place in your organization?

2. If so, in what areas are they operational?

3. If not, are there plans to implement such systems?

4. What trends will impact your organization in the next five years?

5. What conditions might occur as a result of these trends coming together?

6. What is the estimated amount of time in your window of opportunity before the trends culminate into conditions?

7. Please construct scenarios pertaining to the conditions that might occur. What interventions are necessary to be in better control of your organization's future?

8. Is success arrogance present in your organization?

9. If so, what actions need to be taken to avert potential damage that such an attitude can breed?

ENDNOTES

1. Norman R. Augustine, "Reshaping an Industry: Lockheed Martin's Survival Story," *Harvard Business Review* (May-June 1997): 84–86.

2. Vance D. Coffman, "The Imperative of Education for the 21st Century" (Bay Area Council 1999 Outlook Conference, San Jose, California, 15 January 1999).

3. *Reinventing the CEO*, A Joint Study by Korn/Ferry International and Columbia University Graduate School of Business (1989): 1–7.

4. Bill Gates, *The Road Ahead* (New York: Viking, 1995), 89.

5. Lester C. Thurow, *The Future of Capitalism* (New York: William Morrow, 1996), 4.

6. U.S. Department of Commerce, Bureau of Economic Analysis, *Table 1 U.S. International Trade in Goods and Services Balance of Payments (BOP) Basis* (Washington, D.C.: GPO, 21 June 1999), 1.

CHAPTER 3

DynaForces Causing Systemic Organizational Change

Resulting from the collision of the seven impacting trends described in Chapter 2 are the DynaForces, four major conditions I classify as globalization, marketization, informatization, and democratization.

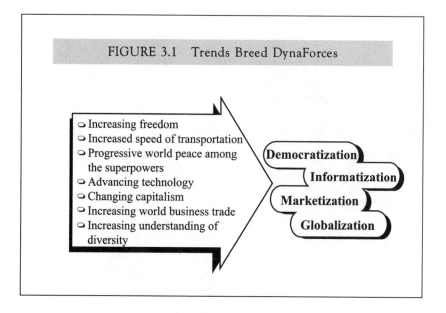

FIGURE 3.1   Trends Breed DynaForces

- Increasing freedom
- Increased speed of transportation
- Progressive world peace among the superpowers
- Advancing technology
- Changing capitalism
- Increasing world business trade
- Increasing understanding of diversity

Democratization

Informatization

Marketization

Globalization

Each DynaForce contains a set of issues that must be managed. Great leaders look ahead and envision these issues. They then work with their intelligence-gathering teams to create possible scenarios of what might happen in their organization at the DynaForce impact point.

GLOBALIZATION

Globalization is the eventual economic, social, and political interconnection of all countries on earth. Just as the United States is the conjoining of independent states, eventually the world will be the conjoining of individual countries. The possibility exists that during the 21st century there will be one world economic unit and an elected world president. However, the world is far from such unity. Globalization generates issues that could become points of conflict, and that, at the very least, demand action. These major issues are:

- Regional economies
- Mobile capital, technology, and labor
- Comparative currencies
- Increased competition

Regional Economies

To become competitive globally, economies are grouping regionally. The world now seems to have three major economies—North America, Europe, and Asia/Pacific.

Eventually, the North American economy will extend into Central and South America to become the American economy, which already influences how we work and live. For example, with the North American Free Trade Agreement (NAFTA) signed in 1993, Mexico, the United States, and Canada operate as free trade economies. Many of the taxes normally paid as trade crosses borders are no longer required, making products more competitive and less expensive. This economic relationship expands the market for an organization's products and services and its potential profits. Even if your organization is nonprofit and does not trade products with these countries, you are nevertheless affected. Your donors will have healthier profits and can give substantially more to your cause.

On the opposite side of the coin, the relationship resulting from NAFTA offers jobs to people in Canada and Mexico that once were exclusive to the United States. Therefore, some jobs may go north or south—mostly south—of our border and eliminate some opportunities for work in the United States. The advantages of this free trade agreement seem to outweigh the disadvantages. Ideas used in NAFTA could eventually expand through South America to make the American economic region an even stronger competitor.

As we move closer to total globalization, an experiment worth watching is the European Union (EU) and the euro monetary unit, which could be the precursor to a potential global monetary unit in the second half of the 21st century. The economic strength of the EU has the potential to grow and be a viable global economic competitor. Because technology is shrinking the world to a virtual capacity, a global medium of exchange will eventually be standardized.

The Asia/Pacific economy is a powerhouse waiting to happen. In spite of economic problems in the 1990s, the economies of the Asia/Pacific region will be stronger in the first decade of the 21st century. China alone, with its 1.2 billion people, offers a tremendous market for other nations' exports. Transnational companies will continue to locate in China for a potentially growing middle class that prosperity will bring and to take advantage of the large workforce. The Asia/Pacific community, in a cooperative relationship, will become a great market for the world's goods and services as well as foster its own export business as a significant percentage of each member country's gross domestic product. This region will be a highly competitive force in this century.

Mobile Capital, Technology, and Labor

For several years, leaders have known that capital, technology, and a country's workforce can travel from country to country—virtually or in reality. Technology allows people to work for organizations across the globe and never leave their home. Throughout the world, banks lend to organizations in other countries. Global capital travels around the world at the rate of over $1.3 trillion per day.[1] The introduction of the Internet has greatly mobilized information, allowing a person to communicate instantly with someone on the other side of the world.

With capital, technology, and labor moving at such a rapid pace, it is important to coordinate schedules around time zones for live communications. For example, workers on a particular project in your organization may actually live in another country and communicate with you via the Internet. To interact with those workers, employees may need to work at night in the United States. Many customer service centers are available for calls at any time. All this mobility will eventually render our planet virtually borderless.

Comparative Currencies

As nations divide into strong economic regions for competitive purposes, we will see vast fluctuations in prices for products and services. This fluctuation will greatly impact jobs and consumer prices. For example, several years ago, when Mexico suffered economic woes, the value of the Mexican peso dropped drastically so that it took many more pesos to buy American products in Mexico. Thus, the market for many of the products exported to Mexico from the United States was endangered because U.S. products became too expensive for Mexicans to buy. As a result, jobs related to exportation of products to Mexico were lost.

The recent Asian economic crisis caused products imported from Asia into the United States to be less expensive. This situation cut into the profits of American companies in competition with Asia because American companies were forced to lower their prices on competing products and services. This in turn affected jobs. On the other hand, it was a great time for vacations. Travel packages to Mexico during the peso devaluation or to Japan during the Asian crisis held some great bargains.

Tying the world's economies to one economic unit is a complex issue. However, one common currency could eventually be helpful. By the time the one-currency issue is resolved, the units traded will be e-currency, for the world is moving swiftly in that direction.

Increased Competition

Increased competition breeds the need for competitiveness and emphasizes investment, productivity, and performance.[2] Organizations the world over will work at reducing the cost and increasing the value of their products and services. The same competitive need will prevail in the workforce. Every member of the workforce, including leaders, must provide an ever-increasing value for the compensation received. In fact, value must exceed compensation. Everyone must continually update their skills to remain valuable. People will become obsolete approximately every two to three years unless they renew their value through continuous learning. Leading-edge opportunities will prevail for those who frequently assess a dynamic big picture and take positive action.

Investment is a building block and measure of competitiveness. The quantity and quality of hard asset investments—machinery and technology—and such soft asset investments as training, education, research, and development make an organization more competitive. These measures of competitiveness are necessary in profit-oriented businesses but are also very helpful in nonprofit organizations and government agencies. For example, many churches are investing in their own high-tech multimedia equipment and are training and educating their staff to operate them. On-site recording studios are becoming quite common; and some churches are even paying for their staff's classes in job-related areas.

Productivity is another measure of competitiveness. Improving the efficiency of production is a key to winning in the cutthroat global marketplace. And wise investments in hard and soft assets also increase productivity. The two go hand in hand. One of the prime reasons that the United States saw such a remarkable bull market in the late 1990s is that organizational leaders made wise investments in research and development as well as in people in the 1980s. These investments increased productivity and innovation and set the United States apart in the fields of telecommunications and technology.

Because of increased international competitiveness, more emphasis will be placed on organizational and individual performance. One model expected to be used in the workplace of the future is the sports professional. On a sports team, players are paid for being good at what they do and for cooperating with the team to achieve a common goal. Contracts are negotiated based on talents and ability with the stars paid very well. Marginal players may or may not make the team. A player is only as good as today's game. What he did last year, even if the performance was stellar, does not matter if he cannot play in the game today. Similar situations will exist in the organization. Leaders will be paid well for great performance. Contracts will be negotiated, but if the leaders are no longer able to perform, they will be cut from their project. Performance will determine each leader's value.

MARKETIZATION

Marketization is the process of responding rapidly to changing market conditions. This particular phenomenon generates four intricate issues:

1. Pure capitalism
2. Private power: performance-based workplaces
3. Rightsizings
4. Emphasis on efficiency, effectiveness, quality, and customer service

Pure Capitalism

The United States exemplifies a capitalistic economy, but its system is a mix of capitalism with some social attributes such as welfare. In an economy characterized by pure capitalism, only the most competitive countries, organizations, and individuals will survive because social props are absent. Entities that deal effectively with the competitive issues discussed under the topic of globalization will succeed in this kind of environment. Pure capitalism that is based on production and profits has the possibility of being blind to such factors as gender, race, religion, and age. The value of leaders in the workplace will be based solely on their ability to perform; in pure capitalism it's winner take all. The questions then become: "What will happen to people who are underperforming in a purely capitalistic economy? Will this particular American economy begin to segregate people by class and divide the population into the haves and have nots?"[3]

Private Power: Performance-Based Workplaces

Business is the most powerful institution in the American economy today. In pure capitalism, private interests dominate public interests. *Private interests* would be investor-owned organizations and *public interests* would be government entities. Nonprofits would be a separate category. We are already noticing that government and nonprofit organizations are taking on many operating procedures similar to those of private businesses. Private business lobbies often dominate some of the decisions made by lawmaking bodies. This was a major campaign issue of U.S. presidential candidate Ross Perot in the 1996 national election.

When private power exceeds public power, many government agencies will be privatized. In this scenario, government employees will be competing against the private sector for employment, and job security will be based on performance rather than on seniority. Thus, workplaces and rewards for employees will be performance based.

Rightsizings

Organizations will expand and contract with the economy. Therefore, the number of workers required will expand and contract as market conditions dictate to the organization. In an expansion mode, employees often want to believe that this situation is permanent. However, when more countries enter the global competition game, more organizations and more people will be competing in the workplace. They will then be a part of what I call the *workplace accordion model*, a model that expands and contracts according to prevailing conditions. So the idea of continuing to be just the right size will be what corporations and organizations will adhere to in the future. The rightsizing movement will be ongoing because in a purely capitalistic economy people flow is as great a concern as cash flow. No one will be kept on the payroll who is not directly contributing to the goals and the profitability of the organization.

Emphasis on Efficiency, Effectiveness, Quality, and Customer Service

Because organizations emphasize efficiency, productivity in organizations is a decisive factor. Efficiency is measured by productivity, and with organizations introducing more information with better tools and technology, productivity per person will rise.

Effectiveness, however, is also important and must be considered. Consumers, not the organization, determine the effectiveness and value of a product or service. In today's marketplace, the organization must measure both efficiency and effectiveness.

Great leaders who orchestrate competitive organizations are also astutely aware of the systems that comprise their industry. They are always seeking feedback on processing time and value to the customer. At the Center for the 21st Century, we define a process as a series of transactions that takes place in the same manner over and over—a series of repeatable transaction loops. Multiple processes then combine to make up a system. Effective organizations are always looking for ways to shorten the process, increase its value to the customer, and increase process innovation.

Leaders of most state-of-the-art universities adopted the systems approach for decreasing student registration time and thus maximizing convenience. Instead of standing in line for hours to register for individual classes, students can now register in most universities 24 hours a day via the Internet. Through the innovative use of technology, the processing time has been greatly reduced, and the students, who are the university's customers, are better served.

Quality is another factor in the marketization process. Inherent in the term *quality* are several ideas—no errors, no returns, accuracy, fast turnaround, and knowledge of the product. In other words, end users of a product or service decide whether the product or service has quality. The end user wants no hassle in using a product or service: the less hassle, the greater the quality is rated by the customer. The hassle factor has become a determining force in the repeat buying of products and services.

Take Amazon.com, for example. Jeff Bezos, its CEO and *Time*'s Person of the Year, is obsessed with customer service. In all his media interviews, he never fails to mention the company's focus on the customer, the philosophy that pervades Amazon.com's culture. When I first encountered Amazon.com several years ago, the first thing I noticed was the ease of navigating its Web site to find the items I wanted. There were vast choices and promise of fast delivery. No sooner had I ordered than an e-mail message gave me the status of my request. Later, a second e-mail message provided another update. Within a couple of days, my book arrived. The price was right and the service was wonderful. From then on, I was hooked. Amazon.com continues offering more products and services, and I keep on buying them. Evidently, others do too. Amazon.com is experiencing a phenomenal sales growth.

Customer service as defined by the end user emanates from marketization. Quality products and quality customer service go hand in hand. Only feedback generated by end users will determine whether they have been served with accuracy, efficiency, effectiveness, and courtesy. All organizations, not just profit-oriented corporations, should be concerned with customer service.

In the highly competitive marketplace, it is a lot less expensive to retain a loyal customer than it is to develop a new one. At the Center for the 21st Century, the cost of doing business with a new client is nine times that of doing new business with a current client, a figure higher than the average. Normally, it costs four to five times more to recruit new business than to secure business from a current customer. According to Randy Robason, global director of Private Client Services for Arthur Andersen, "It is exponentially easier to retain an existing client than to attract a new one. With a current client, you have already developed a relationship. The key to keeping that client is listening to his needs and determining the best possible solution for him."

Every conceivable effort must be made to keep customers satisfied and to encourage them to develop brand loyalty. Customer faithfulness in general is fleeting. Organizations *earn* customer loyalty one day at a time.

INFORMATIZATION

Informatization is the process of extracting and managing knowledge from information. Of all the competencies of U.S. organizations in this high-tech world, knowledge management ranks high on the list. The United States is the front-runner among other nations in its ability to take complex information and then store, manage, and transmit it throughout the world.

In the new century's organization, problems must be solved at the point of contact. Knowledge workers are empowered to seek solutions on the spot. The time necessary to send the problem up or down organizational channels will no longer exist, but problems cannot be solved unless a worker has the information at hand and the skills to organize, understand, and use that information. The greater the worker's ability to convert information into knowledge and manage that knowledge, the greater the value of the worker to the organization. Knowledge is the new organizational capital. Great leaders are responsible for seeing that a knowledge management system is in place and that the workers are skilled in its use.

Informatization generates the following issues:

- Environmental dynamism
- Complex systems
- Virtuality
- Redistributed capital spending
- Increased work complexity

Environmental Dynamism

Possibly more information can be found in today's daily metropolitan newspaper than the information people were exposed to in a lifetime in the 18th century. If people of that century were suddenly dropped into this new millennium, they couldn't cope. And to newspapers add the Internet.

There is an information explosion, in which the elements of our environment are constantly in motion. With ever-changing, anytime, anyplace information, it becomes difficult and almost mind-boggling for us to keep up with changes. We must constantly prioritize the knowledge we need and niche our competencies, continuing to narrow our focus in our area of specialty. For example, many CPAs and attorneys are reducing their expertise to only a small portion of the tax code. As more information is available, there is more opportunity to think about and critically analyze minutiae. With that in mind, it is very important to maintain a global view of our work and lives.

Complex Systems

Earlier in this chapter, I mentioned that multiple processes compose a system. As the number of processes in a system increases, complexity becomes the rule. In today's complicated organizations, systems are constantly reorganizing their parts like an ever-moving kaleidoscope. During the industrial revolution, when systems were much simpler, organizations could measure cause and effect, and greater predictability was the norm. In today's complex world, even the most sophisticated computer simulations often cannot measure the effect of multiple variables on multiple systems, so predictability is limited.

Mathematicians claim that it is difficult, if not impossible, to measure and predict the movement of a pendulum hanging from a moving pendulum. This same difficulty can be seen in the workplace situation of a leader whose company depends on changing marketplace conditions. The leader is like a pendulum swinging from a moving pendulum as his or her work security depends on marketplace conditions and the organization's response to them.

When marketplace conditions change, it is often difficult to predict the exact results on the individual's position. With chaotic conditions in the marketplace, there will be chaotic conditions in the workplace. Leaders must always be aware of the fact that they can be eliminated at any point because organizations will continually be rightsizing. No leader is exempt from this situation—not even the CEO. It is wise to monitor marketplace conditions and become self-reliant.

Information that determines market direction and consequently organizational direction is normally readily available. Great leaders know that not only are their positions uncertain, but workers' positions are also precarious. They advise workers of these issues while making pertinent information available to them. Career centers in such companies as Sun Microsystems, IBM, Hewlett-Packard, and Monsanto help workers become career self-reliant. Each organization's center varies in structure—some are decentralized and virtual while others have a physical location. The objectives of these centers share a common theme, however, in that each career center offers resources for assessing workers' skills and determining workers' strengths and then helping workers gather information on career opportunities for which they qualify.[4]

Virtuality

The term *virtual* literally means *appearing to be but is not*. When I worked in the field of database management in the 1970s, storage capacity was at a premium on the large mainframe computers. A method was invented to overlay capacity so that there would seem to be more storage available. We called that concept *virtual storage—*capacity appearing to be greater than it was. The term *virtual* is used today to depict everything from dishes being described as virtually clean in dishwasher detergent commercials to virtual reality. In virtual reality, we can view a world that appears to be real but is not.

In virtual organizations, a loose relationship can exist among associates, other organizations, suppliers, workers, and customers. Even though these entities don't technically and formally belong to one organization, they appear to because they work together in a very cooperative way. Virtuality is a concept that is here to stay and is made possible through elaborate information technology.

Redistributed Capital Spending

According to the U.S. Department of Commerce, beginning in 1990 there was more capital spending on computers and telecommunication equipment than on the U.S. industrial infrastructure. Many economists and futurists use this figure to indicate that the information economy replaced the industrial economy as of 1990. With more capital spending on communications, information processing, and distribution equipment, the types of work introduced will be much more complex and will require a higher level of thinking ability than exists today.

The Center for the 21st Century believes that by the year 2010, a large majority of the employees in the workplace will be knowledge workers. Great leaders realize that knowledge work takes place on a very different level than does industrial work. An eight-to-five schedule is not possible for knowledge workers. It is impossible to think by the clock; sometimes ideas must incubate for several days. In an industrial world, products are produced on a timely, predictable basis. Knowledge workers deal with innovation and creativity, and with the exception of deadlines, the time factor must be highly variable. With redistributed capital spending obvious, we know that there is a whole new workplace environment being generated.

Increased Work Complexity

Organizational leaders are questioning whether our K-12 educational system is adequately preparing students for the complex work environment that awaits them. I am encouraged to see the numbers of conversations and virtual partnerships that are incubating between schools (both public and private) and organizations. It is only when business and education work together that we can create a workforce that will be able to excel in the 21st century.

Even though unemployment is very low now, many people are underemployed because they have not acquired the skills and abilities it takes to work in a 21st century environment. All workers, not just those who work in high-tech environments, will be required to use sophisticated information tools. Those who are not prepared for this new type of workplace will not be able to participate in the abundant wealth of the 21st century.

"Systems have become a standard of the workplace," states Stephen Katsanos, deputy director of the Office of Corporate Communications at the Federal Deposit Insurance Corporation (FDIC) in Washington, D.C. Mr. Katsanos remembers his early days there when typewriters were used and one central fax machine served the entire agency. Technology was so limited that he would call reporters on Friday evening and read by phone a press release announcing a bank failure. In 1986 he got the first personal computer in the executive offices and began testing electronic batch transmissions. "We then debated the proper ratio of computers to numbers of employees," he explains. "But now in the 21st century, every employee needs an electronic workstation. We not only communicate through fax, e-mail, and the Internet to outside media organizations, but we have a sophisticated intranet for batch distribution across our organization. So information is transmitted instantaneously—internally and externally as well."

Fred Roberts, FDIC's associate director for Training Design and Development, Training and Consulting Services Branch, reports that the FDIC is solidifying a short-term and long-term strategy for information and learning. The FDIC currently assists employees in developing and updating their computer skills by providing online tutorials (CBT) that can be accessed at the desktop. Desk-side coaches offer one-on-one personal assistance and training. A help desk provides telephone assistance with PC hardware and software as well as with telephone, voice mail, and fax problems. Ninety-minute structured coaching sessions on a variety of topics are also available. "Department of Administration (DOA) has piloted a desktop IT-TV program, which should greatly increase the efficiency of employees' capabilities," Roberts explains.

"Our bank examiners conduct a tremendous amount of work online, which is good for them and for the banks. This minimizes the time spent with the banks in the field and allows them to focus on key areas as they visit the individual bank. The use of these key systems improves the process and saves time for all involved," Katsanos summarized.

DEMOCRATIZATION

Democratization is the freedom process toward which most countries are moving. Never in the history of the world have we had so many countries whose people have attained freedom. The transitional period is always chaotic because people are not accustomed to freedom of choice. After the chaos subsides, a redefined society exists.

When communist rule ended in Russia, for example, "men and women educated to work in a top-down command economy found themselves with no jobs, tasks, or salaries," says Sharon Tennison, CEO of the Center for Citizen Initiatives in San Francisco. Soviet institutes across Russia closed their doors—or worse, kept them open offering symbolic salaries. The smarter Russians realized they had to quickly make the jump to developing a product or service useful to the new bottom-up private activity. "The latter developed like the Wild West, with no laws, no models, and no support from governments (local, regional, or federal). Russian citizens who believed business to be evil had no entrepreneurial infrastructures," Tennison explains.

Russian entrepreneurs were thrown into survival mode with no other choices. "They faced corrupt bureaucrats, intraentrepreneurial rivalry and several levels of Mafia. This period lasted roughly from 1989 through 1995 before it began entering a less impossible—though still very difficult—era," she concludes.

In a pure democracy all people have an equal vote. It is possible for small groups to unite to get attention. They can make their point peacefully through harmless protest or they can be more violent through acts of terrorism. In democracies, peaceful protest will often outweigh terrorist acts. As the world evolves, however, we can expect small groups that are trying to become visible to use both peaceful protest and violent terrorism to get attention.

Democratization generates four major issues:

1. Empowerment
2. Individual responsibility
3. Earning/accountability mode
4. Rising entrepreneurism

Empowerment

In democratic societies, as well as in democratic organizations, more power is placed in the hands of individuals. This process is called *empowerment*. In many organizations, empowerment is a major initiative. In fact, throughout the last decade, organizations have increased worker empowerment as their structures have become networks and replaced the more hierarchical forms.

If democracy provides an atmosphere for empowerment to thrive, individuals will have more power and, it is hoped, they will use it wisely. Grassroots movements can take place in an empowered society. People who would not necessarily have a voice can certainly gain more power in a democratic organization or society.

In a social setting where individuals do not have capital or possess marketable knowledge, they obtain power through violence. I contend that violence is powerful, but random violence is even more powerful. If people are not equipped to compete in a 21st century society and have inadequate moral boundaries, violence will perpetuate itself.

Individual Responsibility

In a purely democratic society, individuals are responsible for their own behavior. A law enforcement officer is not found on every corner. Inherent in people within a democratic society is the responsibility to honor the legal code and to act out behaviors that would benefit society as a whole. Individuals are largely responsible for determining the contribution they wish to make, then making that contribution in proportion to their ability. Democracy offers many rights, but these rights must be balanced with responsibilities for democratic societies to survive.

These same principles exist in an empowered organization. Workers are largely self-governing and do not require leaders to police their activities. In fact, self-governed workers are sometimes offended by attempts to patrol their every move. However, for-profit business organizations rarely become purely democratic. If everyone had an equal vote, there would be no overriding vote to handle crises. Great leaders reserve the right to rise to the cause in crisis and take the risk of determining direction. That does not mean that leaders don't intelligently gather data before making decisions. Sometimes, however, the required response time will not allow committee meetings and consensus gathering.

Earning/Accountability Mode

In a truly productive democratic organization, the self-governed have the attitude that they must earn their rewards. Leaders believe that they must earn the loyalty of the workers. Workers, in turn, believe that they must perform to expectations in order to stay in that organization.

For the past 50 years, workers and leaders have increasingly assumed an attitude of entitlement. The thought process was: "I deserve it, and I should have it by default." Workers felt entitled to continue employment with an organization simply because they had been there for a long time. Leaders, on the other hand, felt entitled to worker loyalty simply because they were signing workers' paychecks. Those attitudes shifted during the late 1980s when seniority and longevity on the job no longer guaranteed employment. Workers felt betrayed and lost trust in their employers. Skepticism led to less loyalty. Entitlement attitudes gave way to the earning mentality required for survival in the 21st century.

To be successful in the new century workplace, workers must earn their rewards through daily performance and be accountable for their actions. Good behavior will be rewarded and justice will prevail for inappropriate behavior. Workers must be willing to accept the consequences of their behavior.

Great leaders, in turn, must also be willing to accept consequences. If leaders don't create an atmosphere conducive to worthwhile work, then workers will not feel any inclination to stay with the organization. An ongoing goal of great leaders will be to earn worker loyalty and achieve high performance. Organizational survival will depend on the attitude of its leadership.

Rising Entrepreneurism

In a free society, more people want to be innovative and to go into business for themselves. As freedom is attained, entrepreneurism will always rise. Organizations today are asking individuals to think like entrepreneurs yet participate in teamwork. Entrepreneurial thinking and activities thrive in a free society and are prevalent in organizations that empower their workers. Leaders can summon entrepreneurial zeal from workers through offering organizational grants to explore innovations; giving workers partial ownership of patents; providing workers freedom to explore their own ideas and present them for possible development; and granting workers innovation sabbaticals for coming up with and implementing new ideas.

 LEADERSHIP STRATEGIES

✓ If your organization does not already do business outside its own country, conduct a feasibility study for expanding beyond its domestic borders.

✓ Prepare your workforce to operate globally through training them in international business techniques and teaching them how to do business within various cultures.

✓ Devise a project in your organization that assesses each person's value. This may require hiring a consultant to develop a measurement system. Determine whether the workers' value exceeds their compensation. This assessment should be used on everyone—including yourself.

✓ Once you receive the results of the above project, assign a team to develop a program to increase worker value. Although this assignment will produce new methods, some ideas to consider are (1) using additional technology to increase worker productivity; (2) identifying the training programs each individual needs to increase value; (3) giving small gifts or bonuses to employees as incentives. Contented workers will treat customers well.

✓ If your organization is not doing business via the Internet, form an ad hoc committee to investigate the steps necessary for implementing such an operation. Plan to have at least the first phase of e-business in operation within six months.

QUESTIONS FOR CONTEMPLATION

1. How will globalization continue to affect your organization?

2. If marketization continues to produce a purer form of capitalism and democratization continues to produce more freedom, what are the possible consequences in your organization?

3. Informatization is the most dynamic of all four of the DynaForces. What initiatives should your organization take in order to ensure that a state-of-the-art knowledge management system is in place?

4. What steps has your organization taken to ensure that its workers are career self-reliant? Do further actions need to be taken?

5. Does your organization adequately train its workers to become team-oriented entrepreneurs?

ENDNOTES

1. Jim Landers, "Business without Borders Is the Way of the World," *The Dallas Morning News*, 29 March 1999, 1D. Reprinted with permission of *The Dallas Morning News*.

2. To follow competitiveness issues in major global nations, contact Council on Competitiveness, 1401 H Street, N.W., Suite 650, Washington, DC 20005.

3. More ideas on pure capitalism can be found in the following articles: Richard B. Freeman, "Toward an Apartheid Economy," *Harvard Business Review* (September-October 1996): 114–121; Jeffrey E. Garten, "Can the World Survive the Triumph of Capitalism?" *Harvard Business Review* (January-February 1997): 144–50; Marc Levinson, "Capitalism with a Safety Net?" *Harvard Business Review* (September-October 1996): 173–80.

4. Carolyn Griffith, "Building a Resilient Workforce," *Training*, January 1998, 54–60. Reprinted with permission of *Training* magazine, Lakewood Publications, Minneapolis, Minnesota.

STEP 2

Order the Chaos

CHAPTER 4

Causes of
Organizational Chaos

After studying mathematical models of chaos, I realized that the principles found there could be transferred to an organizational chaos paradigm. Chaos is always a stage of change. Although it is a complex issue, chaos can be explained simply as a state of systemic imbalance. In the past, most work has emphasized how to manage the chaos. Great leaders in this millennium must make a gigantic effort to pre-empt the chaos. The quantum leap for leaders will be from managing in chaos to actually casting a preemptive strike on the tumult so order can be maintained.

THE ORGANIZATIONAL CHAOS MODEL

Let's take a look at the organizational chaos model (Figure 4.1).

Think of an organization as a complex system. Three things can change the complexity of a system—speed, rules, and structure. If any of these factors change, the system will be thrown into chaos. After the chaos subsides, a renewed organization emerges. People who were competitive in the original organization may not be able to adapt to the environment of the renewed organization.

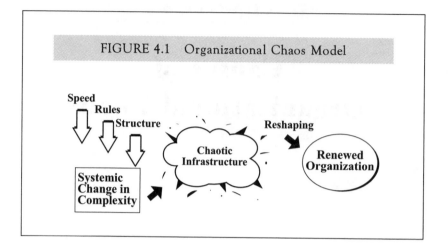

FIGURE 4.1   Organizational Chaos Model

Speed

We are moving from fast to faster, and great leaders realize this. It sometimes seems as if we are living our lives in fast-forward mode. Life cycles of products and people skills are shortening, making the learning cycle much faster. Product development cycles must be quicker. Products must get to the market faster. We have just-in-time inventories and hiring procedures. In this type of organizational environment, we have a project available, hire someone immediately, have that person work the project, and then downsize the person if he or she is not needed anywhere else in the organization. Although this procedure seems cruel, it will be the reality and in fact, is already taking place. The aerospace industry has used this procedure for many years. Virtual corporations are designed for this specific purpose. Contracting contingent workers and outsourcing allow this procedure to take place without affecting permanent employees.

Rules

As organizational rules change, system complexity changes. For instance, when the power in an organization is shifted from one individual to another or from one group to another, the rules automatically shift. Organizations today are changing from very uniform to very diverse. Nations, too, will also be shifting from uniform to diverse.

Changing rules are affecting the way we work. Even the rules for competition will change drastically. Because so much information is available to all competitors, the innovator will be the one who will win. What really happens in innovation is that the rules of the competitive game change until at least one competitor duplicates the innovation. So when an organization changes the rules of competition, that organization surges ahead for awhile.

Structure

Organizational forms are changing. Over the past several years, organizations have moved from a pyramidal structure where power is concentrated at the top to a model of distributed power. In the pyramid structure, employees worked under an old, now outmoded, unwritten contract that implied they had a job at that organization as long as they did their work well, did not make any trouble, and were loyal. We have now moved to a new employer/employee contract, which suggests that workers are more project oriented. As long as their talents and skills are useful to the organization, there will be work for them. When they are no longer needed, then they must look for work elsewhere. Some workers and employers will actually negotiate written contracts just as sports and entertainment figures do today in their professional lines of work.

Another structural change is the move from oversized to downsized, and, I hope, (eventually) to rightsized. Workers in government agencies formerly breathed a sigh of relief when I discussed this issue. They believed that this structural change did not pertain to them. Today, it does. Government agency structures are changing rapidly as downsizing and restructuring are affecting government agencies just as they affect other categories of organizations.

As a result of rightsizing efforts, full employment will move to contingent employment. At the Center for the 21st Century, we feel that a core group of leaders and a few support workers will run an organization much as a head coach and assistant coach orchestrate a sports team. Most workers will be contingent, the majority of them on contract for several years and the minority on short-term agreements. All types of organizations will operate with as little as a 30 percent salaried workforce and as much as a 70 percent contingent workforce. Performance and loyalty will be obtained by working toward a specific short-term goal for which there is a team reward. A similar example is a professional sports team that works together to win each game and eventually the Super Bowl championship. Goals are short term; even the championship is only a one-year goal.

You have probably already noticed that all three of these factors—speed, rules, structure—are affecting a majority of organizations today. Even the church, largely traditional and unchanging, is undergoing vast restructuring. Churches are offering alternatives to staid traditional services. By implementing programs to minister to the whole person, they are meeting the needs of the new millennium's congregation.

The simultaneous changing of speed, rules, and structure, however, catapults an organization into chaos. Normally, if an organization fails, it fails during this turbulent period because it simply cannot adjust to the chaotic infrastructure. In this stage, resources are often inadequate for moving on to a reshaped, renewed structure.

FDIC—a case study. The Federal Deposit Insurance Corporation (FDIC) is an independent agency created by Congress in 1933 to maintain stability and public confidence in the nation's banking system. Until 1989, the Federal Savings and Loan Insurance Corporation (FSLIC) performed a similar function for the nation's thrift institutions. In that year, however, in response to an increasing number of failures of thrift institutions and the resulting bankruptcy of the FSLIC Insurance Fund, Congress abolished FSLIC and reassigned its insurance functions to the FDIC. It also established the Resolution Trust Corporation (RTC) to dispose of the assets of failed thrift institutions. Because the RTC was intended to be a temporary agency with a statutory sunset date, it was staffed mainly by FDIC employees on loan to the RTC. Both the RTC and the FDIC increased their workforces substantially during the 1990s to deal with the increasing number of bank and thrift failures.

When the RTC was terminated in 1995, the FDIC was confronted with the task of absorbing over 2,000 RTC employees, despite the fact that it already had a large and growing surplus of employees in its own workforce as a result of an improved American economy in which few financial institution failures were occurring. The result was the institution of a phased, multiyear downsizing and restructuring program that has reduced the FDIC's workforce by almost half over the past three years. The FDIC's workload for bank examiners was also decreasing, and the organization faced the task of restructuring, finding ways to encourage people to leave, and positioning the organization for maintaining operations with a reduced workload and workforce.

"The FDIC attempted to cushion the impact of the downsizing on employees and to encourage voluntary attrition wherever possible," states Tom Peddicord, an associate director in the Division of Administration who has coordinated a corporatewide workload and staffing review annually since 1996. Downsizing and restructuring are always stressful for employees. However, the FDIC established a staff reduction plan, which included such options as early retirement, buyout offers, outplacement services, relocation offers, and a priority placement program—the Career Transition Assistance Plan (CTAP)—for displaced and surplus employees. Through the options and services offered affected employees, the trauma of FDIC's downsizing and restructuring was minimized.

The FDIC implemented an in-service training program to permit surplus liquidation staff to continue their careers with the corporation by training them to perform bank and compliance examination functions. More recently, the agency has initiated a broad-based program for developing general skills that could be used throughout the corporation. These programs foster more intradivisional and interdivisional mobility as future workload shifts. The training programs give the FDIC a highly skilled staff capable of being mobilized to meet new challenges and initiatives and provide employees with opportunities to develop new skills, often opening up career development opportunities.

Bank supervisory work remains the core of the organization as the liquidation-related activities and the corporation's asset sales force and support staff have declined. The FDIC has consolidated liquidation operations in Dallas, while reducing the number of regional offices across the country. This example shows how government agencies as well as corporations are experiencing structural changes and challenges in the new century.

DEALING WITH CHANGE

There are two ways of dealing with change: (1) a gradual approach and (2) a sudden shift.

Gradual Approach

This way for dealing with change is introduced so gradually that it is hardly noticed. It is phased in little by little until the organization is transformed. Many peaceful social movements use this method to change public perceptions. The group desiring the change may write books, design Web sites, make movies, appear on talk shows, and win key figures over as spokespersons for their cause. Inch by inch, the movement becomes part of the mainstream culture. This type of transition can take several decades.

Many organizations prefer to introduce change gradually. The participants are more accepting if change is phased in one step at a time. For example, I have worked on a church master-planning project. We designed a full building program involving millions of dollars, but we knew that the congregation would never accept the full program at once. So we presented and executed the plan one entity at a time—beginning with expanding the parking lot and ending with a new worship center ten years later.

Sudden Shift

On the other hand, organizations don't always have time for a gradual methodical change. They are sometimes confronted with a sudden shift that throws the organization into immediate chaos. An organization may be operating at a comfortable level of balance when suddenly something upsets the system's equilibrium and catapults the system into chaos. Often, the power structure that had a healthy existence before the upset cannot survive the tumult and therefore cannot adapt to the postchaos environment. A new seat of power emerges.

A good example of a sudden shift is book-buying behavior. In a rather short period of time, Amazon.com's Internet bookstore has been able to develop a formidable presence in the retail bookselling market. Many of the major retail booksellers that have been powerful in the marketplace for decades found it necessary to hurry to conduct Internet e-business to keep up with Amazon.com. Some will survive. Some will not.

Constant innovation will cause industries to experience recurring sudden shifts so that great leaders must become quick-change artists. History indicates that those species and organizations that are most adaptable to the changes in the systemic environment are not necessarily the strongest. Many large organizations will not survive the tidal wave of industry changes now taking place, whereas many small new industries will thrive. Experts are already dividing organizations into two categories: old economy (before Internet commerce) and new economy (after Internet commerce).

Walking through the mire of chaos while allowing reshaping to take place, great leaders are able to look ahead and envision the renewed organization. They have uncanny skill in helping others in the organization to stay focused on the new environment while struggling through the chaos that bridges the old and new organizations. Great leaders inspire hope and excitement in leading people to a better place. Innovation and learning from new experiences are required to remain alive in an ever-changing environment. In the presence of a sudden shift, leaders have two choices—live or die.

CONTROL

Control becomes an important issue during times of change. At a time when there seems to be very little control, it is critical to control all the things we can. As a leader, you are in greater control than you might believe. First, you are in control of intelligence gathering—an assessment of trends, conditions, and issues. Second, you are in control of the choices you make about your organization's future. Third, you are in control of the actions you take.

A major area of control to consider is a preemptive strike on chaos. Because six conditions occur in almost all chaotic situations, it is necessary to anticipate the actions to be taken before these conditions present themselves:

1. A feeling that leaders do not care about those affected
2. Mistrust of information dissemination methods
3. Lack of focus
4. Inadequate resources
5. Lack of preparation for required work
6. Anyplace, anytime, anywhere work burnout

If leaders could predetermine the actions to take before the chaos sets in, then both leaders and workers would be more likely to survive the turbulence.

A Feeling That Leaders Do Not
Care about Those Affected

While I was working with a government agency that was under-going massive change and questioning the people who worked there, all the workers expressed the view that the agency's leaders seemed too preoccupied with their own concerns to communicate with them. That perception was correct. I then asked the leaders what sort of commu-nication tool they would be comfortable using to bridge the workers' perception. Their reply was that the workers would just have to under-stand that the leaders were too busy to deal with them at that time. Wrong response!

During chaos, when people feel a great degree of uncertainty, leaders must acknowledge that they understand. It takes a special leader to lead people through chaos—one that can carry on business with a level head while continuing to consider the people that feel in-secure during the turbulence. To cast a preemptive strike, anticipate this condition before the change is implemented and have communi-cation plans to keep the people apprised of what is happening. These communication modes could be e-mail, videoconferences, memos, videotapes, personal visits to various groups, Web sites, regular meet-ings with group leaders, or an organization newsletter. The main idea is to keep the communication pipeline open: Allow two-way dialogue; answer questions that the people might have.

Workers tell me that they would rather hear bad news properly communicated than no news at all. Living in an information vacuum makes the workforce feel unsafe.

Mistrust of Information Dissemination Methods

Closely related to a perception of uncaring leaders is mistrust of the methods used to disseminate information to workers. When peo-ple feel that information is being purposefully withheld, they begin to mistrust every move that leaders make. Smart people loathe being misled, so morale suffers greatly.

Psychologists tell us there is always an element of secrecy in dys-functional families. Secrets are being circulated that not all family members are privileged to know. This principle applies to organi-zations also. Information withheld eventually throws an organization off balance. Obviously, information is sometimes withheld for security purposes; and to disclose such data would be organizational suicide. What I am referring to is information about company direction, even impending downsizing, that people need to know.

One organization I worked with was preparing to downsize and was moving its operations center to the Pacific Rim. When I asked the leadership when they intended to tell the workforce, the response was that they would withhold the information as long as legally possible so employees wouldn't quit and cause production problems. Not long afterwards workers started hearing a rumor of the impending downsizing via an information leak. Secrecy and withheld information seeded mistrust among the workers, and productivity fell to an all-time low. The gossip grapevine was alive and well; and employees were desperately seeking other jobs. The organization suffered greatly and never again did its workers trust the leadership.

To avoid such a situation, leaders should decide in advance when to share information so as to retain the faith of their workers. An open communication policy breeds trust.

Lack of Focus

Because of the apparent confusion during chaos, workers find it difficult, if not impossible, to prioritize tasks. Great leaders will anticipate this problem and help employees decide what to do and when to do it. In these situations, it is imperative to place tasks into three categories: urgent, important, and critical. For several years, the categories of urgent and important have been used to decipher action priorities. However, with so little time and so many action items that are both urgent and important, I suggest a third category—critical. This classification helps to calculate the impact of leaving an action item undone. If not doing something would cause adverse consequences, then that item would have priority over urgent and important matters.

Many organizations operate in a constant state of chaos because leaders are indecisive. Indecisiveness leads to a constant change in rules and throws the organization into chaos regularly. When leaders fail to set priorities, productivity falls because workers resort to engaging in busywork.

Inadequate Resources

In a strongly competitive environment, resources are tight. Profit margins are razor thin and progressively getting thinner. To keep productivity high, workers are asked to do more with less. To date, the United States has profoundly increased productivity by downsizing people and investing heavily in technology. At some point, however, productivity gains will slow or level off. Then what? The answer: Become inventive.

Organizations must examine all systems they have in place so as to reduce by half the time it takes to process transactions. Great leaders will anticipate this need, communicate priorities to workers, and allocate resources under the best stewardship practices possible. Great leaders do not wait to hear complaints from their workers. They know in advance that more with less is a recurring problem during chaos and will have plans in place to communicate how resources are to be used before disapproval of current procedures is heard.

Lack of Preparation for Required Work

In times of economic boom and expansion, there is little time to train people adequately for the work that is required. Organizations are scrambling to recruit individuals with experience in the type of work needed. Because knowledge workers are at a premium, the human capital is not always available.

Training and development professionals have had to shorten training cycles to accommodate organizational stipulations. In the new Internet companies, CEOs are being hurled into tasks they are not prepared for. An executive may have started out as a computer whiz but now needs marketing expertise as well as an understanding of initial public offerings (IPOs). Then there is a mad scramble to hire consultants and staff to help with the requirements suddenly cast on these new CEOs. The sudden shift to prosperity in uncultivated turf has thrown many new Internet companies into chaos.

Anyplace, Anytime, Anywhere Work Burnout

A high-tech worker recently told me, "I have to be *on* 24 hours per day, 7 days a week. My world is so fast paced that I've become almost addicted to my own adrenaline production. When I have a quiet moment, I look for excitement." As we talked, his mobile phone rang twice, and his beeper beeped three times.

Most workers live in an unprecedented high-speed work world. Because of workers' specialized knowledge, a shortage of workers, squeezed profit margins, and myriad other reasons, workers must be able to be contacted at all times—even while vacationing on a remote island. Leaders have operated in this environment for several years, but this environment exists for all knowledge professionals today. There is no place to hide.

With telecommunication tools such as pagers and cell phones added to laptop and palm computers, the Internet, and intranets, work can be done anywhere. In many cases, there is no requirement for workers to go to the office to work. With a constant need to be in touch with the organization, it is difficult for leaders and workers to retreat and relax. Great leaders will recognize this phenomenon and preempt the burnout that is likely to occur. Such factors as deliberate cross training so that not all people are on call all the time, scheduled times that phones and pagers are turned off, and certain places that are off limits to interruption will decrease the burnout that might occur. I can already hear some leaders say, "I can't let people go off call. That is impossible. We need them in touch all the time." Great leaders recognize that knowledge workers are at a premium. Burnout is detrimental to both the worker and the organization. What was once fun can become drudgery. Forewarned is forearmed.

INTERVENTIONS

If a change in rules, speed, or structure occurs, the six conditions just discussed have a great probability of occurring. Thus, interventions should be designed beforehand, so I have devised a plan described below that I use in plotting interventions. (See Figure 4.2.)

The CE Corporation Case

In Chapter 1, I cited my work at the CE Corporation (a fictitious name), where I was engaged to help the company through changes necessary to make it competitive in its marketplace. Until recently, CE Corporation had had a recurring captive business, but competitors had entered its field, and CE was being forced to move some of its

FIGURE 4.2 Chaos Prevention Plans

Types of Changes:
- **Rules:**
  - ‣ Order takers become salespeople
  - ‣ Survivors take on jobs once handled by downsized personnel
  - ‣ Executive bonus plans changed
- **Speed:**
  - ‣ Rapid training of salespeople
  - ‣ Quick development of market plan and literature
- **Structure:** ‣ Sales and marketing unit created

Method of Introducing Change:
- ‣ Sudden shift—the most flexible and competitive will survive

Uncaring Leaders
- ‣ Meet with all groups to explain circumstances and accept responsibility for company plight
- ‣ Set up career and outplacement counseling for the downsized people
- ‣ Announce downsizing
- ‣ Send salespeople to quality sales training.

Mistrust of information dissemination
- ‣ Open financials to employees
- ‣ Show financial projections in order to assure survivors that CE Corporation is targeting a turnaround
- ‣ Hold regular meetings to review company progress
- ‣ Share new sales and marketing plans with all employees

Lack of focus
- ‣ Meet with the team leaders to prioritize tasks
- ‣ Monitor team goals and accomplishments regularly to keep groups on target
- ‣ Leaders are always available to work with requests for help in setting priorities and for allocating resources

Inadequate resources
- ‣ Implement physical atmosphere for innovation
- ‣ Train people to think out of the box
- ‣ Allocate resources in rank order according to priority
- ‣ Define tangible rewards if goals are met

Lack of preparation for work requirements
- ‣ Conduct a training needs analysis
- ‣ Secure proper training for each employee.
- ‣ In time constraints, ask employees to seek education and training on their own time

Anytime, anyplace, anywhere burnout
- ‣ Design humor into the workplace
- ‣ Define a schedule when people are off from pagers, mobile phones, and e-mail
- ‣ Take a short retreat or play afternoon periodically

employees into sales. In addition, the company was forced to down-size 15 percent of its workforce, reduce the bonus schedule for its exec-utives, and move into smaller office space. These changes had to be made quickly because the corporation was losing money rapidly. The corporate leadership never saw the big picture because they were not looking ahead. The CEO and president didn't see the competitive challenges coming until it was almost too late, so CE was running to catch up.

All of the adjustments caused change in the speed at which CE was forced to move, change in the rules by which the company did business, and change in the original organizational structure because order takers were forced to become salespeople. To control as much of the ensuing chaos as was possible, company officials and I brain-stormed possible interventions for the probable circumstances.

We then filled out a chart like the one in Figure 4.2.

THE PRICE OF CHAOS

With carefully planned interventions, chaos can largely be con-trolled. However, there are times when chaos happens anyway and the tumult can have a disastrous downside. Some people are inexperi-enced in handling chaos and fail to recognize it simply as a stage of change that eventually will pass. They tend to react negatively to the ubiquitous insecurities that chaos introduces. Here are some of the likely negative attitudes or conditions exhibited during the turbulence:

- Concerns about safety
- Economic volatility
- Loss of hope
- Survival mentality

Concerns about Safety

One of the greatest needs of the human being is to feel safe. Dur-ing times of chaos, a perception of insecurity is pervasive. Everything seems so unpredictable. When people feel unsafe, behavioral, rela-tionship, and workplace difficulties often arise. Some important employees may seek work elsewhere out of fear. Stress rises with inse-curity because there is always perceived threat, and there may even be an increase in illnesses and deaths. People's natural tendency is toward balance, and chaos disturbs that balance.

Economic Volatility

An organization in chaos is often accompanied by economic volatility. It's hard to predict profits when the company is operating on a roller-coaster. Nonprofits, religious institutions, and government agencies can also suffer economic instability. When social chaos exists, economic volatility affects the whole of society. For instance, when the government of Russia underwent structural changes, the society seemed to ravel. There were riots, an increase in violence, the closing of many businesses, and people standing in long lines at the supermarket for rationed supplies.

During economic downtimes, when layoffs are prevalent, social issues often come in conflict. With limited funds for government programs, often intergenerational conflict arises over which group should receive funding—the old or the very young.

Likewise, divorce causes chaos in the family structure. More often than not, the family reports economic volatility during and immediately after divorce proceedings.

Loss of Hope

People lose hope when they feel that an outcome will not be positive. So long as there is a chance of a positive outcome, people maintain hope. The greater the probabilities of a positive consequence, the more optimism people have. The loss of hope de-energizes and depresses people. They refuse to move forward, which is why it is so important for leaders to keep communicating a vision of the renewed organization. Never let people lose sight of where the organization is headed. Don't allow the people to focus on the chaos; keep their eyes fixed on the renewed organization.

Great leaders in the past have been masters at inspiring hope. Winston Churchill constantly reminded the English people to never give up during World War II. That inspirational message kept the eyes of the English people fixed on winning the war.

During the Great Depression, President Franklin D. Roosevelt told the American people that fear itself was the only thing they had to fear. He helped Americans stay fixed on the prosperous America that was to come, not the tumult they were in at the time.

Great leaders reinforce hope!

Survival Mentality

People naturally have a survival instinct. In the face of a perceived threat, they move to a survival posture, measuring off turf and acting to defend it. Whether the sense of entitlement is real or imagined, individuals fight to protect what they believe is theirs.

One example of a survival mentality is economic espionage. During the cold war, Americans were well aware that foreign countries were stealing military secrets, a practice that continues today even though the cold war is over.

But spying is alive and well in the corporate world, where the stealing of business secrets is at an all-time high. There are elaborate schemes to obtain competitors' trade secrets—so much so that the Economic Espionage Act signed in 1996 has made it a criminal offense to steal trade secrets. Economic espionage is committed by competitors, employees, and even foreign governments, and great leaders are alert to this type of espionage.

As I have mentioned before, corporations will continue to rightsize to survive cutthroat competition. When people feel that their jobs are threatened, they tend to become territorial. One major way they do this is by withholding information from their colleagues. Competition creates a perception of scarcity. When people believe there are not enough resources for all, they tend to hoard assets for themselves—actually a form of greed. Where knowledge is the wealth generator, people tend to hoard information, the raw material for the creation of knowledge.

When information turfing takes place, the entire organization suffers. In chaos, teamwork and sharing knowledge are the roads to reducing tumult and reaching a more balanced state.

LEADERS BEWARE

Whatever the organization type, leaders must beware of negative conditions and attitudes that can sabotage efforts to lead people to something better. Just as interventions can be designed to order chaos, it is possible to design interventions to prevent negative conditions and attitudes.

Here are some suggestions:

Condition/Attitude	Intervention
Concerns about safety	Train people to become self-governing and entrepreneurial.
Economic volatility	Lock in as many financial controls as possible as a preventive measure.
Loss of hope	Constantly communicate there'll be a renewed organization and better times ahead.
Survival mentality	Have an information-sharing system in place. Reward information sharing. Ensure enforceable consequences for withholding information.

 LEADERSHIP STRATEGIES

✓ Identify changes in speed, rules, and structure that are happening in your organization and formulate specific plans for dealing with them.

✓ Choose the better way to implement each specific change—gradual method or sudden shift—according to the necessary timelines involved. Consider everyone's acceptance, including customers.

✓ Set up a task force to address any worker stress that may result from workplace instability. Direct the task force to identify the potential stress discussed in this chapter, then implement measures to reduce it. These methods may range from time off to a concierge service or a visit to a health club.

QUESTIONS FOR CONTEMPLATION

1. How have the rules changed in your organization?

2. In what ways has the structure of your organization changed?

3. Has the speed increased or decreased in your organization? How?

4. In which manner has change occurred in your organization—gradual approach or sudden shift?

5. Have you designed interventions for issuing a preemptive strike on chaos that involve the six conditions mentioned in this chapter that might occur?

6. Have any of the five negative conditions or attitudes exhibited during turbulence been evidenced in your organization? If so, which ones? How were they handled?

7. Has your organization taken precautions against economic espionage? If so, are they adequate? If not, what needs to be done?

CHAPTER 5

The New Century Organization

It's no secret that the organization of the new century will be very different from the organization of the 1980s and early 1990s. To stimulate your thinking about this new organization, I have listed the old and new organizational rules:

Old Organizational Rules	New Organizational Rules
Organization-dependent employee	Self-governing worker
Lifetime employment	Performance-based ratings
Power at the top	Distributed power
Embarrassment from layoffs	Expected multiple downsizings
One-industry workers	Multiple industry experiences
Upward mobility	Lateral/networked mobility

In the last chapter, I discussed causes of chaos and pointed out the need for interventions so that the organization could exist in an improved state of balance. The more order that we apply to the chaos, the more smoothly the organization runs.

To further order the chaos, we must understand that the structure of effective organizations has permanently changed. Structural change, as pointed out previously, is one of the three precursors of chaos. By understanding the new system and adapting work to thrive in this new culture, leaders are well on their way to ordering chaos. Let's go through the new organizational rules listed above.

SELF-GOVERNING WORKER

After World War II, organizations began to foster dependency on the part of employees. During the industrial age, workers could plan to stay with a stable organization for a career lifetime if they chose to do so. Many people in the past generation have worked for only one organization and have retired from that place of employment with a great benefits package. As the organizational environment became more static and stable, workers became more dependent on the organization to provide their benefits packages, necessary training for advancement, and work assignments. In many cases, workers depended on their leaders to do much of their thinking for them.

The postwar industrial era borrowed two agricultural terms to describe the leadership/worker role. I grew up on a farm, where I heard my dad refer often to our farm workers as the hired hands. When I finished graduate school and joined the industrial workforce, I began to hear familiar terminology. Thinking leaders were called the *heads,* and workers who carried out the orders were known as the *hands.* Has that paradigm changed!

The organization-dependent employee has given way to the self-governing worker (including the leader), who may have uncertain tenure with the organization. This situation exists in business but is also finding its way into nonprofits and universities. Although you as the leader will prescribe training for workers, you will continue to expect self-governing workers to provide some of their own training to keep their skills state-of-the-art. In some organizations, leaders as well as workers are responsible for seeking their own work assignments— mostly project work. In essence, all work is temporary today, temporary being defined as 1 day or 20 years. In all cases, however, no one should consider work to be permanent.

For several years, businesses have experienced intense competition and squeezed profit margins. Downsizing has become a way of life and is beginning to be accepted by the workforce. Although it is a new experience, many workers admit that they are continuing to search for the company that will offer them security for the remainder of their work life. This is not reality. That company does not and cannot exist today. Great leaders ask workers to concentrate on their ability to find work rather than on permanent employment. Great leaders also provide avenues for workers to maintain their state-of-the-art skills through such services as career centers.

PERFORMANCE-BASED RATINGS

Until just a few years ago, seniority with an organization held merit. Now, the ability to perform to and beyond expectations is the topmost work requirement. Compensation and rewards are based on performance, not past experience alone or seniority. Nonprofit organizations, government agencies, health care and educational establishments, and even religious institutions have yet to feel the full brunt of this performance-based workplace phenomenon. Such regulated companies as utilities are in for shell shock as they begin to deregulate. I work with some universities who are questioning the feasibility of professorial tenure. Should there be some performance requirements to remain in tenured status? That question is being explored.

"The issue of performance will become increasingly important in the 21st century," states Richard Chang, the 1999 chair of the board of directors of the American Society for Training and Development. Chang explains that in the past decade most performance management systems within organizations were activity based. Today, the most effective organizations have learned that outcomes and results must be quantified. "There is a critical need to accurately measure results and provide incentives to achieve the highest performance possible," Chang continues. "This is the critical challenge in organizations going into the 21st century."

As CEO of Richard Chang Associates, Chang consults with major corporations on performance issues and processes. He believes that leaders must focus on key results and performance measurement and be certain that this process is aligned and cascaded throughout the organization. Added to the individual's ability to perform specific tasks should be an ability to understand and interpret why things happen. "Great leaders are able to define what those key outcomes are, put them into practice, and set up a proactive measure of success for employees," says Chang, coauthor of *Performance Scorecards—Measuring the Right Things in the Real World* (Jossey-Bass, 2000).

As organizations have moved more into team structures, motivating individuals to peak performance has been more difficult, Chang explains. A multitiered approach for measuring performance works best using methods for near-term and reachable goals while also setting line-of-sight performance measures that are two or three years in the future. Chang cites the example of the salesforce, which most often focuses on volume alone and is often not careful about details in collecting information necessary for customer satisfaction. This behavior causes loss of productivity for support staff and other operational employees and affects the overall profitability of the company. So a multitiered reward approach for the salesforce could include, for example, compensation that is based 60 percent on sales volume and 40 percent on customer satisfaction.

High-performing organizations require high-performing employees. The more effectively an organization manages and trains its people, maximizing their skills, the more successful it becomes. "Linking pay and reward systems to performance is imperative for organizational success," Chang concludes.

DISTRIBUTED POWER

No longer can organizations perform well if all power is relegated to a few people. As I discussed in Chapter 1, leaders emanate from all areas of the organization; and just because they are identified as leaders doesn't necessarily mean that they are at the top of the organization (even if the organization is a modified hierarchy). Knowledge workers must have leadership skills inherent in their work role. Each individual brings special talent and knowledge to the workplace and is the leader in that level of his or her expertise. A baseball team is made up of individuals with special skills who, when working together, inspire the team to excel. The same principle works in other organizations. Individual knowledge applied as a team effort brings strength to the organization.

The Internet is a prime example of the contribution of a multiplicity of knowledge workers with each providing special skills to form a network that is unimaginable—yet it works. Of course, several people had to take the lead to connect the network and to create search engines so that the general public could make sense of the whole thing.

Within organizations, workers will work on intranets much as the general public and many organizations work via the Internet. Power and decision-making ability will be distributed to those workers connected to the network. Self-governance will be a necessary skill for at least three-quarters of the workers in the near future. Robots will

eventually replace many non-self-governing workers who are dependent on strict instructions and job descriptions.

EXPECTED MULTIPLE DOWNSIZINGS

I began my high-tech career in the early 1970s at an aerospace
company in Texas. In those days, most companies were stable,
although it was well known that aerospace companies hired lots of
people when they won a contract and downsized (we called it "laid
off" then) when they lost a bid for a contract. Because the companies
usually downsized on Friday mornings, it was a common joke at my
company that an optimist was someone who brought lunch on Friday.

I remember one specific Friday very well. I had just received my
master's degree the evening before. When my manager called me into
his office, I thought he might be going to surprise me with a raise for
getting that extra education. Instead, I was shocked to learn that my
whole group of 35 people was being downsized that day because the
Texas company's bid had gone to a California company. Amazed, I
asked, "How long do I have—two weeks?" He dropped his head,
rolled his eyes upward, looked at me, and mumbled, "No, you need
to go back to your desk, clean it out, and leave immediately. We're asking your whole group to do that for security reasons."

I could not believe my ears. No job! Laid off! How embarrassing! Next I had to tell my family. The first words out of my mother's
mouth: "What did you do wrong?" That, of course, made me feel
worse. Even in the aerospace industry, where layoffs were common,
being downsized was very embarrassing. Victims of the layoff were
considered by outsiders to be responsible somehow for their plight.
Because most of the organizations in America were stable, people outside the aerospace environment didn't understand the instability of
that industry. Little did I know that 30 years later the entire organizational world would be based on that same model; I had just gotten a
jump start on the downsizing experience.

In the 21st century people may experience downsizing multiple
times in their careers. Because organizations are either directly or indi-
rectly dependent on global markets, projects and work will depend
on the fluctuations of the worldwide stability of the organization's
marketplace. With the proliferation of mergers and acquisitions, organizations are experiencing massive downsizings.

No longer is being downsized an embarrassment but it is now a very common expectation in the workplace. "A great paradox exists," according to John A. Challenger, CEO of Challenger, Gray, & Christmas, "in that 1998 was the worst year for downsizing in half a decade even though the United States was in an economic boom." Many people will experience downsizing multiple times. Wise leaders will always be prepared to find other work and will encourage the organization's other workers to do the same.

MULTIPLE INDUSTRY EXPERIENCES

Whereas people formerly became specialized in one industry, multiple industry experiences are prized in today's organization. Chairman and CEO Louis V. Gerstner, Jr., of International Business Machines Corporation (IBM) was with RJR Nabisco and American Express before joining IBM; and eBay's Meg Whitman worked for Disney, Stride Rite, Hasbro, and Procter and Gamble. These examples depict a broad range of experiences across industry lines.

Valued résumés at one time reflected years of repetitious experience. Now the best résumés reflect years of multiple experiences. In many organizations, college and high-tech training are enough to land someone a well-paying position. Today's marketplace is somewhat contradictory in that specialization is required, yet a global perspective is necessary. With multiple industry experiences of workers and leaders characterizing the organization, the operational paradigm changes. We are beginning to witness the blending of organizational models.

LATERAL/NETWORKED MOBILITY

Upward mobility has been replaced by lateral or networked mobility with less room at the top. By necessity, however, there must be a top. Even in networked organizations, someone must assume the ultimate leadership role, especially during a crisis. In urgent situations, normally there is no time to call a committee meeting or seek consensus. Quick decisions must be made by a leader willing to take immediate action. Under normal conditions, however, consensus building and teamwork are important.

With the continual flattening of organizations and increase in self-governing knowledge workers, compensation will be based on individual and team results. Base compensation and bonuses will be patterned after the sports team concept. Many organizations today are even providing hiring bonuses much like signing bonuses in the sports world. In the knowledge domain, professional recognition and increased compensation will be rooted in how well workers perform specialized tasks and the degree to which they are effective in interpersonal and team relationships. The increase in the contingent workforce will cause the networked organization to be more feasible.

QUALITIES OF THE NEW CENTURY ORGANIZATION

In this new millennium, such organizational shifts as those just discussed will continue to evolve. We know there are three elements that great leaders are called on to manage:

1. Dynamism
2. Empowerment
3. Virtuality

These three organizational elements are generated from the DynaForces discussed in Chapter 3.

Dynamism

Organizations are animated—always moving and changing in markets, people, and processes.

Markets. Lockheed Martin is a survivor in the world of market change. Peter B. Teets, president and chief operating officer, stated the following at a recent AeroEngineering Conference:

> We experienced firsthand the rapid consolidation of the defense portion of the aerospace industry. Lockheed Martin itself represents the melding of 17 separate heritage companies. Collectively, we closed 16 million square feet of plant space and eliminated more than 100,000 posi-

tions. As a result of those—and other—actions, we are now saving our customers $2.6 billion annually in reduced costs. A decade ago, the Department of Defense represented some 90 percent of the sales of our heritage companies; today, Lockheed Martin relies on the Department of Defense for only about 50 percent of our business . . . . Competition is a never-ending aspect of our business—so the question becomes: *How can we compete more effectively in the long run?* The answer is simple to state, if not so simple to implement: *enhance intellectual capital.* In other words, invest in people—find the *best and the brightest,* give them plenty of development opportunities, and keep investing in them throughout their careers . . . . *Intellectual capital* really means that people are the bottom line.[1] (Emphasis added)

Markets are also swiftly changing for religious institutions. Thinking of churches, parishes, and synagogues as having a market was once considered heresy. Yet growing churches have realized they do and consistently strive to reach their target market. They make adjustments to their methodology in order to change as their market changes. A good example of such a phenomenon is the Willow Creek Association (WCA) in South Barrington, just outside Chicago, Illinois.

In 1992, the Willow Creek Community Church created the Willow Creek Association. It's mission is to inspire, equip, and encourage Christian leaders to build churches that reach people who do not attend church. It has since become an international network of outreach-oriented churches. "The goal of the association is to provide the kind of leadership and encouragement that pioneering churches need to prevail in their efforts to lead people to Christ," says Harvard MBA Jim Mellado. Under his leadership, the WCA has grown to more than 4,700 churches from 25 countries. One of the many things that makes the WCA unique is that while most traditional denominations are falling apart at the seams, the WCA has created a unified organization with representation from more than 80 denominations worldwide. Its August 1999 Leadership Summit had 5,000 in attendance in South Barrington and another 5,000 attended via satellite at 11 remote locations. In 1999, attendance at all its conferences exceeded 60,000 people.

"Willow Creek Community Church (WCCC) and other WCA churches are a hotbed of ministry innovation," says Jim Mellado. "The Willow Creek Association distributes that ministry innovation to other churches and church leaders. People want insight, innovation, and to be effective. When a ministry breakthrough occurs at WCCC or other WCA churches, we want all churches in the Association to benefit. That's why I think more and more churches are joining the WCA. If churches are serious about becoming more effective, we are here to serve. As we serve these pioneering churches, they provide leadership to many more churches beyond our reach."

When asked how WCA was able to be so successful at crossing denominational lines, Mellado replied, "We are focused on the implementation of the core things that unite us: the Great Commission/ Commandment (referring to Mark 16:15 in the Holy Bible), and not second- and third-level issues where we might disagree."[2]

Finally, markets are changing for government entities. Yes, governments have markets, too. Government markets—the people they serve—are demanding more. For example, Dallas has a separate number, 311, for people to call with questions and specific requests. That allows 911 to be used solely for emergencies. Because citizens are becoming more assertive in demanding good customer service, government entities must change continually to provide better assistance.

People. People cause an organization to change. New entrants into the workforce today are mostly women and other minorities according to the U.S. Department of Labor. Leadership gradually is shifting to later-born baby boomer executives and Generation X executives. Leaders of many of the new Internet companies are in their late twenties and early thirties. And now members of Generation Y are beginning to enter the laborforce. With all this diversity, the mix of labor and leadership will change the focus and values of work. Balancing work and family life is a primary requirement for retaining highly skilled workers. People who don't feel they are spending enough time with their families will look for a workplace whose culture values their life outside work.

With different cultures in the workplace, many people are asking to practice their religion at breaks and at noon. Certain religious groups wear special attire that they want to wear to work. Organizational policies must adapt to this changing environment. Chapter 10 discusses contracting the whole person—not just one's skills—to attract and retain stellar performers. The religious cultural change in the workplace is also discussed.

People will be in constant motion in the 21st century workplace. Individuals will flow in as their work is needed and will leave when their tasks are completed. Leaders will not always be leading the same people and will not have the time to get to know their employees very well. Leaders must be astute at ad hoc interpersonal relations.

Processes. In successful organizations, processes are constantly in a state of transformation. Whether the process is customer relations, training, or marketing, organizations are always looking for more effective and efficient methods. One of the primary functions of a great leader is to be on the outlook constantly for new and better ways of executing processes. Health care organizations, for example, are continually tightening their processes to adapt to the squeeze on fees imposed by the U.S. government and insurance companies.

As systemic changes occur inside the organization, between organizations, or among organizations and customers, dynamism takes place. The constantly changing environment cries out to be managed—and moreover to be led.

Empowerment

In the early 1990s, empowerment became a buzzword. Most companies gave it lip service, but few actually empowered their people. Since those early years, the collapse of hierarchies has forced leaders to recognize empowerment as a necessity—not a novelty or employee benefit. In an empowered organization, strength rests largely in workers who are equipped with the necessary knowledge and are able and willing to accept the responsibility of self-governance. Great leaders know that their role is to make resources available so individuals can function to their potential and the organization can maintain a competitive edge.

Until the 1990s, many organizations were using industrial age management techniques derived from the theories of Frederick W. Taylor, a mechanical engineer. That is amazing in that Taylor's work began in 1890 and spanned the first half of the 20th century. Taylor believed that management (used in this context as synonymous with leadership) planned, organized, orchestrated, and controlled every detail, and that the worker was to be forced into a corporate structure.

He was opposed to a worker's having motivational incentives. Taylor espoused a very predictable systems approach wherein cause and effect were easily measured and controlled. The worker was treated as a piece of machinery whose efficiency was all that mattered.[3]

Many organizations continue to exercise control over workers to the point that people feel devalued. Taylor's scientific engineering has evolved into human engineering, focusing on the individual as a human being, but human engineering still denotes a degree of control and manipulation. In many organizations a misconception continues that putting the emphasis on people empowers workers when, in fact, most organizations have not yet reached their empowerment potential.

With the advent of knowledge work, however, each worker knows his or her task better than anyone else does. Making decisions at the point of origin is much better than outside task boundaries. Workers are asked to be entrepreneurial. Instead of their identity being defined by the company, workers are being asked to think "out of the box." Leaders must adapt to having their actions and philosophies questioned by workers. In fact, because of this questioning attitude, workers in some cases are considered to be contemptuous. The very qualities that could have gotten a worker fired 20 years ago are considered assets today.

Virtuality

In Chapter 3, I introduced virtuality, an issue generated from the DynaForce informatization. As discussed, virtuality is that which appears to be real but is not. In our research at the Center for the 21st Century, we have discovered that real is in actuality traditional. For example, a real office is one that has a physical location, typical in the late 1800s through today—in other words, a traditional office. A real corporation traditionally was headquartered in a building where people gathered daily to work, but as a result of communication technologies, we can now redefine where work is done and how work is structured. Today, technology provides us with the means to configure virtual offices, workplaces, corporations, communities, and even such virtual institutions as universities, churches, and health care facilities. Virtual will eventually become that which is real. What was real, or traditional, in the past will become historical.

Let's take a look at some applications of virtuality. This discussion is not exhaustive. You can probably think of additional examples.

Virtual offices. Offices can be configured from almost anywhere, but the majority of virtual offices are home based. Workers do work from home regularly or for just a few days per week. Larger companies furnish a computer, fax, phone lines, desk, and any other equipment needed to work. Communication with fellow workers happens via e-mail, chat rooms, telephone, teleconferencing, and periodic contact meetings at headquarters or company retreats. Leaders of some companies even make house calls to visit employees on the job.

A variation of the virtual office is hoteling. In this setting, space (usually a workstation or desk) is set aside for the use of multiple people. These areas can be reserved by the hour or by the day. Some of these offices are even personalized for each individual who reserves the space so that it will give a sense of ownership.

Satellite offices are spaces that employees use at remote locations. Usually, the location is away from the more expensive headquarters. Designs vary with some elaborately furnished and others sparsely and inexpensively furnished.

"Anywhere" offices are also quite common. Many people work anywhere with only a laptop, fax, cellular telephone, and pager. Most consultants and account representatives have anywhere offices in order to operate from their clients' offices. Many organizations feel that their employees are only doing real work when they are servicing their billable clients.

Virtual offices allow flexibility. Workers who adapt well to such an environment are self-motivated and excellent time managers. Because there is no controlling boss to supervise their work, they are expected to produce results. That's what they're paid for. People who value freedom enjoy this option. Some people even choose to work in parks and on mountaintops. They take their laptop and mobile technology to a spot that is conducive to relaxation and creativity and work for long lengths of time. They can set their own hours and speed of working. All that is required is that they meet their goals and due dates for projects.

Virtual offices are a viable option for people who don't like to waste time commuting or who wish to be with their family during the day. This option is causing a resurgence of what was once termed a *cottage industry.*

"At Arthur Andersen we find that virtual offices work quite well for many of our employees and clients," says Randy Robason, global director of Private Client Services. "However, everyone in the organization must understand employee requirements for specific job assignments prior to implementing the concept. We here at Arthur Andersen have found that explaining the steps necessary to guide employees through the process is most important in such management changes."

Arthur Andersen, a business unit of Andersen Worldwide, is a global professional services organization with a personnel of more than 52,000 with 363 locations in 78 countries. It began using virtual offices about five years ago and now uses them in all its offices and in many of its lines of business. "Virtual offices are not appropriate for all employees and all tasks," Robason continues. "It requires a great deal of thought and flexibility to be successful, but rewards for both company and employees are significant. The key is that you involve employees as well as management throughout the process, make sure the goals are clear, and that you have buy-in. That way everybody wins," Robason explains.

Virtual institutions. Universities are using cutting edge information technology to deliver education throughout the world. Some of these institutions are in no way traditional campuses. Take Walden University: For a graduate program, it connects top content specialists worldwide with students via its own electronic network. Through a partnership with Indiana University, students can access the graduate research library. Other than some residency requirements, the graduate degree can be obtained totally through the Walden Information Network. Student Ali Naddafpour, CEO of ABS Accounting and Business Services in Los Angeles, says, "Walden has given me the opportunity to achieve both personal and professional growth. Flexibility is of great importance to individuals like me who are actively participating in the business world. The program is providing me with a strong set of tools to improve my hands-on management skills."

Currently, many universities are offering courses on the Internet, and online groups continue to drive the market for learning, such as OnLineLearning.net, the University of Phoenix Inc., Caliber Learning Network, Inc., and Washington Post Co.'s Concord University School of Law in Los Angeles.

How can virtual health care institutions work? In acute cases, people continue to be confined to a hospital if one is available. However, space age technology allows doctors to be in one location and medical facilitators to be in remote locations administering health care. This has important implications for isolated parts of the world where expert medical treatment has been heretofore unavailable.

"In the past, medical treatment and therapeutic facilities have been centralized in hospitals and rehabilitation centers. Patients have had to go to these hospitals and centers or wait in doctors' offices, often traveling many miles for health care. But technology is changing the medical field and may allow the house call to return to mainstream medicine with the transportation of data rather than people," says David C. Balch, director of Telemedicine and the Center for Health Sciences Communication (CHSC) at East Carolina University (ECU). "The actual practice of telemedicine began in the late 1950s. However, the recent upsurge in medical costs, along with technology advances, are now making telemedicine a widespread medical choice."

Telemedicine is a growing health care capability in rural America as well as in prisons and military hospitals. The distance learning program at ECU began in 1989 over a statewide network that links major universities in North Carolina. ECU's School of Medicine began conducting telemedicine consultations in 1992 when Central Prison, the state's largest prison, contracted with ECU to provide telemedicine services. To date, ECU has completed more than 3,000 consultations in 34 different medical specialties over its Rural Eastern Carolina Health Network (REACH-TV). Supporting telemedicine, distance learning, and continuing medical education, the REACH-TV Network is made up of ATM, TI, microwave, ISDN, and POTS (plain old telephone service) communication links spread out over North Carolina.

Director Balch continues:

> Many applications of emerging technologies are under development. Specialist physicians will be able to live any-where, see patients online from anywhere, and provide medical treatment globally. Surgical experts can train and monitor surgeons in other locations using real-time audio, video, and data links. Biosensors of all kinds are being developed to monitor patients anytime, anywhere. These devices will become miniaturized and integrated with tele-communication systems, making them more wearable and adaptable to the individual's lifestyle. These medical innovations will greatly impact health care in the 21st century.

An interactive medical and wellness Telemedicine kiosk is currently under development for commercial deployment in the Rapid Prototyping Lab of ECU's Telemedicine Center. The kiosk is designed to allow consumers to seek health care at their work site, hotel, shopping mall, or airport. A patient walking up to the kiosk could use a secure health smart card to allow the health care provider access to the patient's medical records. This ability will not only enhance the quality of patient care but will also reduce costs for both the patient and the provider. For HMOs, it will provide increased access to care and decrease the frequency of such high-cost medical environments as emergency rooms. This kiosk is being jointly developed by Telemedicine Technologies Company and The Global Telemedicine Group.

According to Balch:

> Our telemedicine program will continue the integration of patient information and management tools into its network. In addition, we will begin to test and implement virtual reality in the telemedicine environment. The program will continue to expand its hybrid network into rural hospitals and medical centers and will also expand telemedicine into the home with its new TeleHome program.
>
> Health House is a concept jointly sponsored by Telemedicine Technologies Company, Application Valley, Inc., and the Smart House, Inc., a subsidiary of the National Association of Home Builders. Health House will have a smart toilet that can both take a urinalysis and send it to the doctor's office. Another feature of Health House is a smart medicine cabinet that can dispense individual doses of medications or provide reminders of needed refills. The homeowner can set up a doctor's appointment, call up the doctor's office from his desktop computer at the appointed time, and talk face-to-face with his physician. The doctor can then e-mail a prescription to the pharmacy for pick up or delivery.

Virtual corporations. In some cases, a corporate headquarters may not exist. The company is merely a network of people working from separate locations. With this configuration, which is conducive to people flow, people are normally given the independence to choose where they work. When a contract is signed with a client, independent contractors are brought into the network; when the project ends, the contractors leave the network. The number of workers at any one time will vary depending on the amount of work to be done. These workers can be located anywhere in the world. Their organization is connected completely through communications technology.

An example of another type of virtual organization is a temporary company formed with employees of two permanent companies to administer a contract. For example, a computer company might team up with a transportation company to develop an automated transportation system in another country. Employees from both organizations would be assigned to work on this contract, which might last four years. At the end of the four years, the employees would return to their original companies.

Quite often a virtual organization is composed of a company's supplier and the company itself with the inventory system available at both companies. This type of organization allows the supplier to store inventory and the company to act as though it has the inventory in stock—a cost-cutting measure for the customer that allows just-in-time inventory.

Some of the most successful examples of virtual organizations are the ones in e-commerce. eBay is the world's largest *personal* online trading community: Personal not only because it is used by individuals—not big businesses—but also because the company believes that each customer is someone who deserves to be treated with respect.

Pierre Omidyar, founder and chairman of eBay, launched the company in September 1995 as a result of a conversation with his wife. An avid collector of Pez candy dispensers, Omidyar's wife commented that it would be great to trade with other collectors online. To fulfill the need for efficient, one-to-one trading on the Web in an auction format, eBay was born. Customers can now buy and sell everything from collectibles to computers using eBay, which provides millions of new auctions and thousands of new items every day. If it's unique, you can probably find it there.

Virtual reality. Remember that earlier in this section I predicted that virtual would become real? Well . . . here it is—virtual reality—in its primitive stages. I can wear specialized computerized headgear and go to unbelievable places, an ability useful for travel agents in taking clients on trips before they actually embark. Realtors will be helped as prospective homebuyers can actually feel as if they are touring a property that may be thousands of miles away. There are countless uses for virtual reality—from entertainment to serious medical treatment of people living on space stations.

Virtual reality, however, goes further according to author and inventor Ray Kurzweil, winner of the 1994 Dickson Prize, Carnegie Mellon's top science award. In his book *The Age of Spiritual Machines: When Computers Exceed Human Intelligence,* Kurweil claims, "Later in the 21st century, as neural implant technologies become ubiquitous, we will be able to create and interact with virtual environments without having to enter a virtual reality booth. Your neural implants will provide the simulated sensory inputs of the virtual environment—and your virtual body—directly in your brain."[4]

LEADERSHIP STRATEGIES

✓ Make certain that all workers have been made aware of new workplace rules and have been trained in how to follow them.

✓ As a favor to workers, emphasize that each is ultimately responsible for his or her own career, although the organization will serve workers in every way possible to make the workplace pleasant and productive.

✓ As a leader, maintain your own state-of-the-art skills at all times. Be prepared to exercise alternatives in case you are the victim of a downsizing.

✓ Deliberately maneuver your career to gain multiple types of experiences. Develop projects that force you to exercise varied leadership skills.

✓ Document accurate quantitative records of all projects you are responsible for. Among other things, be able to show increases in productivity, revenue, and profits as a result of your leadership.

✓ If your organization does not have a compensation and reward system for knowledge workers, take the responsibility for initiating such a system.

✓ Encourage workers to assert their ideas and question your motives. In turn, be prepared to back up your decisions with a sound basis for your judgments. Expect workers to "talk back" to you.

✓ Explore all avenues for developing a virtual environment to increase productivity. Be aware of feelings of isolation that can occur when workers are in remote environments. Set up regular conference calls with them and talk with them yourself or delegate that responsibility to someone else. Also provide them with technology such as Internet chat rooms and e-mail, intranet services, and even videoconferencing capabilities, if affordable, so that they can be in contact with coworkers.

QUESTIONS FOR CONTEMPLATION

1. Is your organization playing by the new organizational rules discussed at the beginning of the chapter?

2. If not, what actions do you suggest to update the organizational rulebook?

3. Please review the discussion of the theory of Frederick W. Taylor in this chapter. List any ways that your organization is continuing to employ his ideas. Should changes be made?

4. In what ways could your organization implement virtuality to increase productivity?

ENDNOTES

1. Peter B. Teets, "Investing in Intellectual Capital—The Key to Engineering Achievement in the 21st Century" (paper presented at the Aviation Week/CEF AeroEngineering Conference, AeroExpo 98, Long Beach, California, 17 November 1998).

2. Reprinted with permission of the Willow Creek Association (www.willowcreek.com).

3. Milton L. Blum and James C. Naylor, *Industrial Psychology: Its Theoretical and Social Foundations* (New York: Harper and Row, 1968), 575-78.

4. Ray Kurzweil, *The Age of Spiritual Machines: When Computers Exceed Human Intelligence* (New York: Viking Press, 1999), 144.

CHAPTER 6

The Role of the 21st Century Leader

Because the 21st century organization is dynamic and characterized by empowerment, virtuality, and globalization, 21st century leaders will play by a whole new rulebook. In order to make the transition from the 20th century static, command-and-control, reality-based, domestic organization, new millennium leaders must have a totally different mind-set. In this chapter, we look at some concrete ideas for effective new century leadership.

LEADING THE EMPOWERED ORGANIZATION

To create an empowered organization, leaders must understand, provide for, and support those they lead.

Understand. Great leaders must understand individual motivation, group dynamics, power distribution, and convergent leadership.

It is important to know how people feel and to understand what builds self-esteem. In the past, it was uncommon to tune into people's feelings. Psychologists are realizing that intelligence about our own as well as others' feelings is a cornerstone in peak performance. Feelings are temporary and momentary, so the leader must be astute enough to pick up changes in personality during interpersonal transactions.

People need to feel valued in the workplace. Sometimes they need to lead, at other times to follow—depending on the work assignment. People like to win; they like choices and the ability to reach their potential. Great leaders work with people to see that their desires are satisfied. Work assignments can be structured so that individuals' needs are met.

Group dynamics is a science in and of itself. Because effective and efficient teams are the avenues through which organizations become competitive, the study of groups is an important element in understanding leadership. Every group has at least one emergent leader who will determine group behavior. Some in the group will be influenced by the group's collective behavior, which is why social movements seek out key individuals to advocate their cause. Others in the group will be influenced by what the leader thinks.

Power distribution exists on a continuum. If the leader makes the decision, then the leader is in control. If the workers make the decision, then the workers are in control. Most decisions are made somewhere between the two extremes. Together the leader and workers define boundaries for decision making, then make judgments accordingly. In some cases, leaders ask for suggestions and make a decision based on those recommendations. In other situations, leaders ask the workers to make a team decision and the leader approves it. In an empowered environment, leaders defer most decisions to the people actually working on the tasks. Power is distributed according to the situation.

Convergent leadership is a term we use at the Center for the 21st Century to describe the simultaneous management of crisis and development. Before the 1980s, most growth was gradual and developmental. Crises were handled, then leaders went back to the business at hand. In the present organizational environment, leaders must forge ahead with a convergent model in mind.

Historically, leaders have specialized either in crisis management or in growing and developing organizations. Depending on organizational needs, leaders were hired for their expertise in one or the other area. Now leaders must be skilled in both areas to meet the demands of dynamic organizations. The list below shows the contrasting qualities of the old millennium unilateral leader and the new millennium convergent leader.

Old Millennium Unilateral Leader	New Millennium Convergent Leader
Boss	Coach, mentor, teacher
Power conscious	Worker conscious
Authoritarian	Flexible, participating
Security oriented	Risk oriented
Works in hierarchy	Works in networks/teams
Isolated from workers	Almost zero managerial distance
Expects worker loyalty	Earns worker commitment
Conservative	Enthusiastic, open, inspiring
Dignified	Energetic, spontaneous
Tough	Tough and tender
Analytical	Analytical and intuitive
Interested in employee skills	Interested in the whole worker
Delegates communication	Communicates directly
Avoids media	Courts media
Takes calculated risks	Takes risks in almost total uncertainty
Informs	Listens
Makes timely responses	Makes rapid responses
Status derives from position	Status derives from working hard

Provide for. For workers to perform with excellence, leaders are expected to provide necessary physical resources, including a decent budget for accomplishing necessary tasks. In addition, the following are needed for effective empowerment: common mission/message, perceived stability/consistency, state-of-the-art work assignments, trust, and an atmosphere conducive to intimacy/bonding.

Leaders are responsible for communicating the organizational mission, or purpose, to all workers. The mission should be able to be explained in ten key words or less, preferably five key words or less—almost like a sound bite. In new organizations, leaders develop the mission with the workers, but most people are hired after the organization has been inaugurated. Thus, the mission is communicated rather than developed. But mission statements are altered from time to time, so workers should be involved when statements are changed.

The leader is also responsible for providing a message that communicates common organizational values. Leadership behavior must be consistent with the message. If the message embodying the corporate culture proclaims that all workers are important, then the leader must live up to that message by making people feel significant. If the resounding message is that positive ethical character counts, then the leader must exemplify integrity.

Although organizations might be going through turbulent changes, great leaders create an aura of stability. How can this be done with chaos occurring all around? It's a perception—not a reality. Great leaders inspire stability because they seem secure in their decisions and choices. Stability and consistency are contagious. It's not that the organization is stable but that the leader is stable; the workers then feel more secure and hopeful, which promotes better performance.

State-of-the-art work assignments provide employees with increased expertise. Knowledge workers realize that their position is temporary at best. They use their work as a training ground for their next work assignment. For example, high-tech individuals want to work in companies that have the newest technology, so they are always preparing for the next position or the next company. Understanding that it is their responsibility to remain employable, they seek organizations that provide training and development that will increase their performance capabilities. The development of worker expertise is an effective retention tool.

Great leaders are expected to provide an atmosphere of trust. During change, trust is often the first to go. People begin to build invisible walls around their turf and refuse to share valuable information. This often leads to the demise of a successful organization. Knowledge cannot be managed if there is little trust, and leaders foster trust by being trustworthy. Then workers emulate the message. Great leaders never do or say anything that casts doubt on their trustworthiness.

A challenge for leaders is to create a milieu in which there is emotional intimacy and bonding. This is difficult to do with constant people flow, but intimacy and bonding can be achieved by communicating as openly and as honestly as possible. Take time to visit personally with as many workers as possible to find out what they care about—their families, their hopes and dreams. Listen. Really listen. Then, at what you consider the proper time, show an interest in those things they have shared with you.

Support. In an empowered organization, leaders support workers but do not rescue them. Resources are made available to help workers reach their goals. I had the privilege of sharing the speaking platform at Indiana University with Paul H. O'Neill, chairman and CEO of Aluminum Company of America (Alcoa), which *Fortune* repeatedly names the most admired company in the metals industry. O'Neill told the audience that he travels untold miles every year all over the world visiting Alcoa's workers and listening to them. One question he always asks is, "What can I do to help you?"[1] Then he acts on their requests.

Further support is expressed when leaders work with people to mutually determine performance criteria and reward systems. When workers have input into their performance measurements and the manner in which rewards are distributed, they become stakeholders in their own destiny.

Supportive leaders allow the free exchange of ideas. In fact, they foster brainstorming sessions in which no ideas are blocked, where there is total freedom of expression. Workers are urged to make decisions and carry them out. They are also allowed to experience the consequences of their decisions—both negative and positive. Of course, errors will be made, but rather than punishing the worker responsible, the situation is considered a learning experience.

The Center for the 21st Century often works with new entrepreneurial organizations. We have determined that the first year is one of learning and training with inevitable trial and error. In the second year, company trends start to be revealed, and then entrepreneurs can better determine what works and what doesn't. In the third year, a decision usually is made to continue growing the company or abandon the whole idea.

These same principles also apply to self-governing workers. The timeline may be different, but there is always a learning curve involved in entrepreneurial activity among workers as well as leaders. Leaders realize that this learning curve exists and allow errors to become learning experiences.

Worker autonomy is important in an empowered organization. Flexibility in scheduling, prioritizing tasks, and organizing and allocating resources create a sense of ownership. Workers enjoy working in an organization that allows them to participate in making the rules.

LEADING THE VIRTUAL ORGANIZATION

With virtuality, leadership takes on a new twist. Great leaders must operate with greater purpose. In the traditional world, organizational qualities that we take for granted are no longer there. The physical organization that automatically created a sense of physical community won't exist in a virtual organization. Workers will be isolated and segmented unless strategic policies are in place to bring the community together. People need and want to belong to a community, but many report that the virtual office creates in them a feeling of being disconnected. Astute leaders recognize the existence of this feeling and create a system where unity and a sense of the corporate culture are felt. Leaders must also stay focused on the organizational mission and see to it that members of the network do the same.

Here are some suggestions for leadership in a virtual world.

Connect with Purpose

- All parties involved should be connected with systems that can communicate seamlessly with each other. Recommend standard software packages. Everyone should have access to the Internet.
- If your organization does not have an intranet, explore creating an intranet that privately serves each worker.
- Make certain that workers are connected by cell phones, faxes, pagers, and voice mail.
- Consider setting up extranets with vendors to facilitate mutual data flow.

Communicate with Purpose

- Provide each worker with e-mail and Web page addresses, telephone, fax, pager, and other necessary numbers for all other workers in the network.
- Send e-mail messages regularly to each person in the organizational network.
- Make certain that all workers know the capabilities of all others in the network so all can draw on others' expertise.
- Set up a central online information source so that all network members will have access to the same data.

- Standardize all necessary forms and modes of communication.
- Establish a standard manner in which learning experiences, including errors, are entered into the central system so that others may access the information.
- Encourage open expression of conflict in chat rooms. Mediate network conflict with resolution as a common goal.
- Set up regular teleconferences and conference calls, and schedule chat room times to provide regular group interchange.
- Occasionally schedule retreats, if economically feasible, so that people can interact in person.
- Endeavor to emulate informal coffee break communication by implementing deliberate break-time conversations via chat rooms.
- Continually communicate organizational culture through case studies in e-mail messages or a standard company online newsletter.

Allocate Work with Purpose

- Create a database, after securing worker permission, detailing each person's competencies, values, personality traits, and preferences so that work can be assigned accordingly.
- Match team members through similar and complementary traits to maximize team chemistry.
- Devise ways, such as online retreats and reporting sessions, to keep workers focused on the organizational mission—especially when workers are assigned to a virtual corporation involving other companies.
- Resolve turf wars and polarization issues that often occur when separate cultures are combined.

LEADING THE GLOBAL ORGANIZATION

One of the DynaForces, globalization, is so pervasive that it has become a stand-alone organizational quality that cannot—and must not—be ignored. Even if you lead a small domestic organization, you are affected by globalization. What is happening in other countries influences your products and services whether or not you acknowledge the fact. Globalization is two-way. It involves both the expansion of your organization to other countries and the invitation for other organizations to operate in your country.

Chapter 3 pointed out certain macroissues associated with globalization. In this section, I will address reasons that organizations choose to globalize and points to consider when they do.

Three Reasons Organizations Choose to Globalize

1. Globalizing to expand the customer base. On the consumption side of the equation, it is hoped there will be a growing middle-class market emerging in other countries. As third-world countries become more prosperous, their citizens will spend more money on everything from better foods to makeup and soft drinks. These consumers provide a ready market for many products and services that the United States has had for many years. With the market for such items maturing here, organizations are extending to untapped areas.

More countries will be receptive to imports as democracy spreads. Such countries as India, Taiwan, and China will collectively become gigantic consumer markets as they prosper from their trade with the remainder of the world, especially the United States.

Other than an increase in consumer profits, organizations wish to go global to spread their risks. When an economic downturn occurs in the United States, European or Asian/Pacific economies may be expanding. The majority of U.S. profits would then come from other countries. When the situation shifts, these companies are flexible enough to garner profits from more prosperous countries. Global diversification can prevent a company from suffering a total economic downturn. That's smart business.

2. Globalizing to gain access to the global labor pool. On the production side of the equation, there is pressure to increase productivity. For the last two decades, American companies have been moving their manufacturing operations to other countries to cut labor costs. Approximately 30 percent of U.S. manufacturing takes place outside the United States.[2] If all other factors remain constant, a decrease in labor costs brings an increase in profit margins.

This transference of manufacturing has reduced production costs mostly at the factory level. In the near future, there will be transference of higher-level knowledge workers to a global labor pool.

Because of the paucity of such talent in the United States, compensation is very high, even for new college graduates. At this point, the United States is leading the economic boom in telecommunications and computer technology. However, as other countries grow more competitive, the United States must find a way to reduce labor costs, which is why it will turn to the global labor pool readily available via the Internet.

An increasing number of people from other countries are being educated as engineers, scientists, and professionals in every field. They can work from their own countries in a virtual way via the Internet for a lower relative compensation (holding inflation constant for means of comparison) than is being paid today. For competitive reasons, U.S. companies increasingly will turn to other countries for its knowledge workers.

The global labor pool can also lend valuable and unique expertise. A large percentage of the scientists and engineers being educated in the United States are from other countries and may return to their homeland to practice their professions. Nations such as Singapore are promoting online work options for their labor force and, in turn, wish to connect to the labor pool in the United States.

In many cases, and for whatever reason, workers from other countries are more productive than American workers. However, there can be a marked increase in productivity from recruiting internationally. Robert Gilliam, assistant superintendent of School District U46 in Elgin, Illinois, recruits teachers from Spain, Puerto Rico, and Mexico to work in the multicultural environment of the district. He reports outstanding results considering that 64 different languages are spoken in the Elgin schools and notes an increase in overall productivity as a result of his international recruiting.

3. Globalizing for competitive advantages through partnering. This reason for going global pertains more to governments than to other types of organizations, but everyone benefits. National, state, and local governments promote economic development to enhance specific economies. Even small towns are organized in such a way as to promote their community in other countries. Sometimes specific tax incentives are offered to companies to entice them to locate a plant or other business in a town, which creates jobs and expands the economy of the community. In effect, governments and international businesses create a partnership.

In turn, economic development entities from other countries court U.S. businesses to create jobs that strengthen their economies. The byproducts of this global interchange greatly affect all entities, whether they have attempted globalization or not. For example, if a large Toyota plant locates in a small town, an opportunity to build new schools and supermarkets is provided. The housing industry will grow, thus providing more construction jobs. Local government services will by necessity expand. Nonprofit organizations in the town will, it is hoped, receive more donations. Obviously, the benefits are numerous.

Two Considerations When Going Global

1. Make understanding others a priority. Whether you lead an organization that employs people from other nations or your organization has an office in other countries, it is important to understand other cultures. People's values and beliefs differ. Habits and values may even be tribalistic. And work values may differ from those promoted by your corporate culture. It is difficult to impose one culture onto another and expect full cooperation.

I had a personal experience with cultural differences in Puerto Rico. Like most Americans, I am very time-conscious. I was scheduled in San Juan to give a speech at 9:00 AM and had made my plans accordingly. I would speak one hour, listen to other speakers, then leave on a 1:00 PM flight back to the United States. I appeared in the auditorium at 8:30 AM, but no one was there. Nine o'clock came and went; and still no one was there. I began to look at my schedule to see if I was in the right place on the correct date. Yes, I was. Ten o'clock, still no people in the auditorium. Panic set in. I then wandered outside the building to see that my audience was congregated around a breakfast buffet having a wonderful time.

I approached a member of the audience. "Am I mistaken?" I said. "Wasn't I scheduled to speak at 9:00 AM?" He questioned, "Puerto Rico's time or American time?" Misunderstanding, I replied, "Puerto Rico's time, I guess, since we are in Puerto Rico." "No, no, no," he quipped. "Puerto Rico's time means plus or minus two hours. We don't have to be exact. You Americans are too intense. Loosen up. We'll be there after a while." He was right. At 10:30 AM the audience gathered in the auditorium and we started the 9:00 AM session!

It is also imperative to understand the monetary policies of the country in which you locate a company. Such things as tax and exchange rates, trade policy, welfare programs, pension and legal systems, and health care administration all affect compensation packages—and profits.

2. Adopt a global operating philosophy. Leaders must ask questions such as these:

- Who will lead the organization in other countries?
- How do we intend to expand the organization?
- Will we manage the organization with a holistic or segmented approach?

Some organizations prefer to station their own leaders in other countries when their organization expands. Others encourage positioning leadership from the same cultural background. The decision seems to be based more on organizational philosophy than on a global rule.

Numerous organizations expand through partnerships within the country in which the organization is doing business. Training companies in the United States often seek a partner in a target country, which provides a quick introduction to the culture and specific business operating requirements, and the partners share the profits. Other organizations prefer to expand through mergers and acquisitions; a good example is the merger of DaimlerChrysler.

How the global economic schizophrenia experienced by most organizations is handled becomes part of the organizational philosophy. Some organizations prefer to segment the company into regions and let each region rise or fall on its own. Others prefer the cohesiveness of a holistic approach. When one area of the world is weak, the profits from more successful areas are used to bolster the trouble spots until the economy experiences an upturn in that region.

LEADERSHIP STRATEGIES

✓ If you have not already done so, enroll in a personality dynamics course so that you can better understand people's motives and behaviors.

✓ Appoint a task force to keep abreast of state-of-the-art technology. Implement that technology for better recruiting, retention, and productivity.

✓ Make certain that you are operating as a new millennium convergent leader. If you have any characteristics of an old millennium unilateral leader, devise a plan to change them.

✓ Begin to phase in a virtual workplace. Lead it with some of the suggestions in this chapter.

✓ If you lead a global workforce, make certain you understand different cultures and incorporate those cultural differences into your training of workers who must interface internationally.

QUESTIONS FOR CONTEMPLATION

1. Please look at the table in this chapter depicting the characteristics of the old millennium leader versus the new millennium leader. What characteristics do you and your organization's other leaders exhibit? Are any of your leaders (including yourself) operating in the old millennium mode?

2. Are the leaders of your organization effective in leading an empowered workforce?

3. In what ways are the leaders in your organization connecting, communicating, and allocating work in a virtual environment?

4. How is your organization involved in globalization?

5. How do your organization's leaders exercise global wisdom and operating philosophy?

ENDNOTES

1. Paul H. O'Neill, chairman and CEO of Alcoa. Information provided by Alcoa.

2. Charlene Marmer Solomon, "Brace for Change," *Global Workforce* (January 1999): 7. Reprinted with permission of ACC Communications/*Global Workforce*, Costa Mesa, California. All rights reserved.

STEP 3

Blend Multiple Organizational Models

CHAPTER 7

Profile of the 21st Century Workforce

To visualize a snapshot of their organization's future, great leaders seek the answers to three key questions:

1. Who will make up the 21st century workforce?
2. What behaviors and values will workers most likely exhibit?
3. How can new ways of working be designed to mutually accommodate both the organization and the worker?

WORKFORCE COMPETITION

Gender Balance

According to the Bureau of Labor Statistics, the current workforce is made up of approximately 47 percent women and 53 percent men. I estimate that by the end of the first quarter of this new century the percentages of men and women in the workplace will be equal. Except during World War II, today has the highest percentage of women in the workforce ever recorded. The ramifications of such gender balance are awesome. There will be intense integration of work into life. The boundaries between work and other areas of a worker's life will be nearly invisible.

Men and women will share home responsibilities more equitably. Up to now, the woman has continued to bear most of the home-based duties—caring for children and the elderly and admitting repair people. However, if both husband and wife are at work, who steps in to handle these responsibilities? The employer, that's who. According to a 1998 survey of more than 1,000 U.S. companies by Hewitt Associates, a management consulting firm specializing in human resources, 87 percent of businesses surveyed offered childcare and 15 percent offered sick/emergency childcare programs.

The duty of caring for elderly parents has fallen largely on daughters and daughters-in-law. Again, the employer will step in with elder day care centers and referral services for care of the aged, services that have been available in larger companies for several years, but the needs will become more acute. At the Center for the 21st Century, we feel that some companies will even supplement the cost of housing elderly parents in a retirement center or nursing home. The costs, even though hefty, are less than the costs of lost productivity of highly paid professional workers. Eldercare is a growing problem as baby boomers' parents and even the 78 million baby boomers themselves are aging. As a result of gender balance in the workplace, responsibilities formerly relegated mostly to women will be shifted to the organization, which will in turn largely outsource the services to various institutions and entrepreneurial firms.

Because many 21st century workers grew up in homes where parents were not always available, they have a passion for being available to their children and participating in their children's activities. Flextime and job sharing will be common in order to provide parental release time.

Extended leave is another option offered by business. Pressure will be exerted to extend the time allowed in the Family Leave Act. This pressure to provide more time off in a fast-moving performance-based environment will complicate planning for allocating work to projects and will further fuel the thrust toward hiring more contract labor. With contract labor, time off will be taken by workers between contracts rather than become the responsibility of employers.

Planned sabbaticals will be more the norm. Again, larger companies will offer these, and independent workers will adjust their leaves to fit life-planning strategies. Workers entering the workforce in their early twenties and staying until their sixties, according to the industrial model, will experience extreme burnout because of the intense pressure of knowledge work. With both husband and wife in the work world, periods of retreat and leisure must be programmed for emotional and spiritual renewal.

We already are witnessing the fact that organizations are offering all kinds of services to families. Concierge services plan everything from barber appointments to elegant dinners. The tight labor market combined with the need to raise productivity is fostering the offering of these benefit packages. The Families and Work Institute's *1997 National Study of the Changing Workforce* indicated that employees with supportive workplaces and higher-quality jobs were more productive.[1]

In my seminars, I often offer this caveat to workers: The myriad employee-offered benefits are helpful and enticing but downsizing is alive and well. The independent workforce is growing by the hour. Take care not to become too dependent on fringe benefits because at any point workers may need to reassume the responsibilities now carried out by corporate concierge services.

Large numbers of single mothers, especially minority single women, exist in the workplace. Nearly one in five employed parents is single and, of that number, 73 percent are women.[2] Quality primary childcare and backup childcare will be major concerns for this group. Assuming the roles of mom, dad, breadwinner, and the family's sole support takes its toll in stress on these courageous people.

Gender balance also contributes to women having more responsible leadership roles than in the past. However, gender balance alone will not cause women to be elevated to leadership. Another contributing factor will be the fact that power is gradually shifting to knowledge workers, and women comprise a great percentage of the knowledge worker base. Because knowledge worker success is measured by degree of competence, women will achieve an even playing field with men. That's why all wisdom points to women becoming a very powerful force in the workplace, especially after the year 2020.

Ethnic Mosaic

According to the *Kiplinger Washington Letter*, between the years 1998 and 2013, 70 percent of retirees will be white and 33 percent of new entrants into the workforce will be nonwhite.[3] A mosaic workforce will eventually be created with neither white nor nonwhites making a majority. Leaders who are accustomed to a dominant workplace culture will face unprecedented challenges.

Organizations have attempted to teach diversity issues for the past decade. However, EEOC filings for race-based discrimination continue to rise. Is diversity training inadequate? Or are people merely insensitive to others? Of course, there are cultural differences. Some cultures are more laid back than others. A majority of Americans, in contrast, are driven to work hard and long hours. Men as a group may exhibit certain behaviors that women as a whole don't tend to exhibit. Biases may exist against people who graduate from certain universities, while at the same time some people feel that alumni of other universities are arrogant. Stereotyping people because they belong to a specific group can be dangerous.

Great leaders realize that they set the attitude regarding diversity that will be followed in their organization. All the diversity training in the world will not take the place of a leader's example.

The leader then must communicate with each individual—try to find out his or her concerns and issues and reveal yours. Work on finding a resolution to the problem of bias and seek some common ground—steps that should be introduced on a companywide basis. Yes, diversity—individual differences—is a reality. Beyond diversity, however, can be unity. That is the ultimate goal.

Our differences will not be the discriminating business issue 20 years hence that it is today. Informatization plus cutthroat competition derived from the cross-impact of democratization and marketization will result in workers being contracted solely on the basis of their performance potential. That's the bottom line.

Varied Household Types

Many baby boomers grew up in a traditional household, with Dad as the primary breadwinner. Mom stayed at home in suburbia to nurture two or three children. Television shows as well as advertisements in the 1940s, 1950s, and early 1960s reflected this traditional type of household that is no longer dominant today. Large numbers of workers presently in the workforce have never experienced this traditional household, which 20 years from now will not even be considered traditional.

During the next decade, households will become quite varied. My list is not exhaustive but here are some other household types that I foresee being represented in the workplace, all of which will be increasing in number. Some 21st century household types are the following:

- Married heterosexual couples with children
- Married heterosexual couples without children
- Single people without children
- Single people with children
- Cohabiting heterosexual couples without children
- Cohabiting heterosexual couples with children
- Cohabiting homosexual partners without children
- Cohabiting homosexual partners with children
- Grandparents raising grandchildren
- Blended families
- Multiple single people, one household
- Multiple families, one household

Because these diverse living arrangements have an enormous effect on employee benefits, distributing benefits equitably is a major issue. Concerned leaders will initiate fair policy—first, in consideration of the workers and, second, to prevent litigation.

VALUES AND BEHAVIORS

Generations

We paid little attention to generational groups until the post-World War II baby boomers came on the scene. By the time all of them were counted, nearly 80 million folks were found to have been born during the 18 years between 1946 and 1964. Leadership roles today are played mainly by the boomers and the last quartile of the World War II generation (whose birth dates were 1923-1945). By the year 2005, leadership will be mostly composed of baby boomers (born 1946-1964) and Generation Xers (born 1965-1976). Increasingly, leadership is becoming younger. Even members of Generation Y (born 1977-1987) are beginning to be represented in such Internet companies as those in e-commerce and in new software gaming and animation—businesses in which Generation X is still dominant, however.

Values

Debates continue about how we acquire our values. Social psychologists are sure that impacting events, which we experience while growing up, have a decided influence on our value systems. For example, the Great Depression of the 1930s is still talked about today by those who suffered during those hard years. Holocaust survivors vividly recall the horrible torturous memories. Each generation has one or more impacting events that shape how they lead and how they view work.

I don't believe in stereotyping people. I believe in looking at individuals as the unique human beings they are. But because I do not know each person in the workplace, I have to make some generalizations. Let's take a look at typical generational values.

Pre–Baby Boomers

The Great Depression and World War II largely influenced this group that was born after World War I. Both impacting events were periods of fear and scarcity that engulfed the whole world. Very few women had worked outside the home but, during World War II, women went to work temporarily while the men went to war. When the war was over, most of the women vacated the workplace to again become homemakers, and two-parent families raised most children. Much of the world was still agricultural; in the United States, the South was mostly agricultural until the early 1950s. These circumstances influenced the values that leaders from this generation brought into the workplace. They believed in hard work and in saving money for contingencies.

Security was very important, as many people had seen their parents go jobless during the Great Depression and never wanted that to happen to them. Job security became the byword espoused by unions and advertised by companies. Workers wanted to hire on with a company and grow with that company until retirement—maybe even stay there 40 or more years.

It was important for workers to be secure in their retirement years. When companies were stable, they provided defined benefits plans that guaranteed income for the years when employees could no longer work. When health care benefits were first implemented, employees were excited to have the insurance company pay most of the hospital bills. Before World War II, hospitalization was little known in the workplace. On top of that was disability insurance paid to workers when they were unable to work in the years before retirement. Social Security, workers' compensation—the list goes on. The key word in all this is *security*—the reduction of fear—for a generation that wanted to feel safe. As workers, they depended on their companies for job security; as leaders, they wanted to guarantee job security and felt they had failed if they couldn't. This is the generation that set up the old employer/employee contract that served well for so many years.

Many leaders of the 1950s, 1960s, and 1970s—even into the 1980s—served either in World War II, Korea, or in Vietnam and hence the implementation of the militaristic command and control, hierarchical corporate power model. Many leaders of that era referred to their employees as *the troops*. The hierarchical structure, in which concentration of power was understood and accepted, worked well for that generation.

Pre-baby boomers were loyal to God, country, family, and their employer. The spirit of cooperation was a cornerstone of the pre-baby-boom generation. Very few people protested being drafted into World War II and fought because they believed it was the right thing to do.

The roles of women were pivotal. Females accepted narrow career choices, and most of them felt that their major role was to be a wife and mother. Men believed that their major role was to be the family breadwinner. In many cases, men were embarrassed if their wife worked outside the home, which meant men could not support their family. With that generation, the male's ability to provide an adequate living was a matter of pride. With the exception of a few women, females had very little power in the workplace—nor did other minorities. The white male was in control.

The pre-baby boomers created the structure that defined for 50 years how work was done and power distributed. In reality, many organizations continue to use that model today, although figuratively they give lip service to having flattened their organizational pyramids.

Tom Brokaw has termed the pre-baby-boom generation the *greatest generation* and has written a book by the same name.[4] I have heard him in numerous interviews compliment this generation on its hard work, sacrifice in wars, and its help in building the United States into an economic powerhouse.

Baby Boomers

World War II was over. Americans were celebrating victory. The United States entered a period of tremendous prosperity. Families moved to suburbia. Record numbers of babies were born. Enter the baby boom generation.

Competition became the theme of this era. Classrooms were filled beyond capacity, and whether students were competing to be picked for the football team or the star role in the senior play, many competed for few positions. When baby boomers graduated from college, it was an employers' market. Again, many people were competing for fewer entry-level jobs. Thus, one value that baby boomers acquired was the belief in competition as a precursor for reaching a goal.

Not only are male baby boomers highly competitive, but this generation's women are highly competitive also. Females targeted positions in professions that were not traditionally "women's work." Female baby boomers dared to challenge the organizational glass ceiling, and some even broke through it.

Higher education was readily available to the baby boomers, many of whose parents from the pre-baby-boom generation went to college from funds available through the G.I. bill. The value of education was emphasized to baby boomers.

More than any previous generation, boomers have focused on careers as an avenue to a satisfactory life. Their work is a source of emotional reward. Success is determined by how far and how fast they move up the organizational ranks, and progress is measured by the degree of their professional growth.

This generation of boomers rebelled against two values held by their parents—material conservatism and loyalty to those in power. Material things are meaningful to many of them, who engage in conspicuous consumption. They spend a lot of money on cars, houses, second homes, vacations, and dining experiences.

During the 1960s, a large contingent of boomers, mainly the better educated, protested against the Vietnamese conflict—although those who fought say it was a *war*. Their parents had supported World War II and Korea without question, but at the opposite extreme many boomers refused to participate in Vietnam and dared to question the wisdom of the U.S. government.

Two major values held by many in the boomer generation that followed them into the workplace were (1) intense competitiveness and (2) mistrust of authority–the legacy of Vietnam. Baby boomers are driven to career success: They are highly competitive; they are willing to take risks to reach their goals. Questioning authority, they are willing to be innovative and experimental, promoting entrepreneurial activities within the organization. They want workstyles to fit their lifestyles.

The last half of the baby boomers were more emotionally affected by the energy crises of the 1970s than the first half. In addition, the corporate downsizings of the 1980s emotionally influenced those born after 1960 because they happened at the beginning of their careers or totally disrupted their parents' lives with layoffs. Consequently, this particular subgroup of the baby boomers is less loyal to the organization than the other subgroup born between 1946 and 1960.

Because of the demands of this generation and rapid-paced market needs, the organizational pyramid began to flatten, and nontraditional ways of working shifted the organization paradigm forever.

Generation X

In many cases, Generation X–those born 1965 through 1976– is not too pleased with the baby boomers, believing boomers wasted resources, left a large national debt, a Social Security and Medicare debacle, environmental problems, and a plethora of social issues for Generation X to manage.

Generation X might also be called the *baby bust* in that births dropped off significantly when it came of age. Impacting events during the formative years of Generation Xers gave way to economic and social instability and family uncertainty. The national economy was schizophrenic. Energy crises destabilized the country. Divorce increased. Dual career parents became the norm. Single parents multiplied. Many members of Generation X were latchkey children, staying home alone behind locked doors a few hours a day while their parents were at work. These social events had a definite impact on the values of this group, values that in turn have been transferred to the workplace.

More than any previous generation, this age group requires a balanced life from employers. Having viewed their workaholic baby boomer and pre-baby-boomer parents, they refuse to sell their whole life to the company in exchange for organizational compensation. Leisure means a great deal to Generation Xers; they program it into their regular schedules. Family time is also important. Because most members of Generation X are composed of dual career parents, they expect their workplace to adjust to their schedules. They are willing to work hard but also want to attend their children's school events and sports activities. Reflecting the work values of Generation Xers is the 1993 Family Medical Leave Act, which allows up to 12 weeks of unpaid leave for child adoptions or births, or illness of the employee or their spouse, child, or a parent.

Generation Xers are able to set firm boundaries. They will say no to work assignments that seem unreasonable or if the work impinges on their free time. Because of a tight labor market, employers defer to this attitude. Worker loyalty is at an all-time low largely because of Generation Xer's mistrust of authority figures. They feel that because many of their power figures have disappointed them in the past, they need to be responsible for themselves in the workplace. They exert great effort in exchange for compensation but don't feel they will be with the organization forever. Those who are prepared for lucrative 21st century careers will fare well under the new employer/employee contract.

Commitment can be difficult for Generation Xers, many of whom have chosen to break tradition and cohabit with their partners before marriage rather than marry without having lived together first as has been the custom for centuries. That lack of willingness to commit has carried over into the workplace.

This is the first generation to be largely computer literate. Because of their experience with technology, Generation Xers are securing well-paying positions and can thus afford an opulent lifestyle. Because they will risk working with a startup company for a lower salary plus stock options, Generation X has produced more workplace millionaires more quickly than any other generation.

Generation X workers are likely to choose an employee organization for its social value, for they are very much concerned with wasted resources, and they disdain industries that abuse the environment or workers' health. Social and work/life issues mean as much as financial rewards in their work environment. They welcome workplace diversity and are more tolerant of gender, racial, and religious differences than were previous generations.

Generation Y

New to the workplace, this group continues to evolve, as most of its members are still in their teens. Generation Y represents another baby boom, so it too will probably have a significant impact on society and the workplace.

This generation's formative years were characterized by more social violence with destructive weapons than has occurred in any previous generation, moral crises in powerful places, and extreme stress in schools. This generation has witnessed the mass introduction of the Internet, which is as revolutionary as the advent of the automobile and television. It has been exposed to an intense education about such serious social issues as abortion, AIDS, unprotected sex, drugs, and alcohol. Instilled into this generation is the power of personal choice, as evidenced by the prevalence of home schooling.

Members of Generation Y are more tolerant of individual differences than are members of any previous generation. They have grown up in schools where as many as 90 or more different languages and dialects are spoken. People representing almost every life choice are seen in the public schools.

Because most of Generation Yer's parents work outside the home and record numbers of their parents are divorced, this group is more self-reliant than any other generation. They feel the need to take responsibility for their own life and are more willing to live with the consequences of their own behavior.

This generation believes in self-expression. During the interviews with teens after the Columbine High School shootings in Littleton, Colorado, I detected the traits used to describe the students killed in the massacre: they were genuine, passionate about life, and really cared about people. I believe that these qualities expressed during those interviews reflect the values of a majority of Generation Yers.

This group is applying some of the social idealism of their baby boomer parents and recycling the social and political conservatism of their pre-baby-boomer grandparents. Easily bored because they grew up on fast-moving animation and computer games, they expect the same adventures in life. Traditional stand-up lectures in school and church lull this group into deep sleep. They are not afraid of expressing themselves as individuals. They find rigid rules difficult to follow—many are habitually late to work, for example. They are in tune with their skills and talents and know how to channel those abilities into life and career choices.

Generally, national politics disappoint members of Generation Y. They don't feel the need to engage in heated political discussions as did their baby boomer parents. Social issues are more important to Generation Yers.

Growing up with computers at home and in school, Generation Yers are technology savvy. Many members of this generation have worked part-time in high tech in their midteen years because employers recognized their expertise. The economy has been generally good during their years, so their expectations of continued prosperity will be unusually high. Their crises have been more social than economic.

Translating these observations to the workplace, Generation Yer's values will fit right in with the new organizational paradigm. It's as if members of this generation have been preparing all their life for the workplace of the future. They will bring a sense of independence and passion for innovation. Because they are easily bored, Generation Yers will thrive on the fast-moving, global organization and will be excited by the virtual environment.

Family will be very important; hence the continued emphasis on work/life balance. Generation Yers will integrate their work into their life to such a degree that the two will become one.

Generation Yers will be a refreshing addition to the workforce. The pendulum is swinging back to task commitment, concern, passion, and genuine caring for the rights of others, thus fostering natural, rather than enforced, teamwork. There will be a move away from the self-centeredness of the past two generations.

NEW WAYS OF WORKING

Now that we have viewed a snapshot of the workforce and understand their behaviors and values, let's examine the work structures and processes that will mutually accommodate both the organization and the new worker.

We already know that the organization must operate to maximize profits—or whatever it designates as its measure of success. Workers want state-of-the-art work, excitement, varied duties, flexible schedules, and tasks that promote social value. Added to that, people desire emotional and perhaps financial ownership of their work as well as participation in the financial ownership of the organization. Last but not least, workers want very attractive compensation packages.

Meeting Individual Workers' Needs

Great leaders recognize the new values being introduced into the workplace and seek to maximize work processes and assignments. First and foremost, respect is to be paid to individual traits, expertise, and workers' personality. Great leaders enter into dialogue with workers and ask what they prefer. Because some people would rather work in a virtual environment, that should be worked out if possible. I have recommended hoteling and telecommuting to several clients who refused to establish a virtual environment because of the initial expense of the technology. Five years from now, they will see that an investment in restructuring would have been well worth the cost. Many workers, however, are not productive in an isolated technology-driven environment, so these individuals should be identified and grouped into a more intensive social setting.

As Generation Xers and Yers increasingly dominate the workforce, they will resist control and authority, so tasks must be designed with these workers in mind. Expected outcomes will be mutually defined, making the worker an accountable stakeholder and the leader a supportive coach. After tasks and outcomes are agreed on, designated checkpoints should be established; between checkpoints, workers are on their own. There must be mutual trust between leader and worker for the work process to succeed.

Although teamwork is promoted and expected for the organization to thrive, we know from the profiles presented earlier in this chapter that the majority of people, especially the baby boomers and Generation Xers, tend to be self-centered. It is public knowledge that the baby boomers were the *me generation*; and some observers have even termed Generation Xers as the *more for me generation*. Great leaders coach people to develop their individual skills and professional expertise, then base rewards on improvements achieved on an individual level.

Balancing Teamwork and Independence

Because of the power of teamwork in organizational success, however, leaders must arrange workspace for collaborative efforts and arrange the work itself so that each person, when making his or her most expert contribution, produces a necessary part of the whole. Additional rewards are given for the team's projects at completion. Ideally, competition is fostered between organizations, not within the organization, which is why rewards are given for individual improvement and not on the basis of comparative performance. The greatest reward, however, must be given on a team level—something that can be achieved only through cooperation.

In the future, the need for independent contractors will increase. Because of the increasing demand for work/life balance, many dual career couples will opt for individual contractor status. It is common knowledge that temporary, contingent, and other freelance workers are on the rise. Thus, as the organization moves largely to just-in-time employment, new generations coming into the workforce will prefer that workstyle. Because of the anytime, anyplace work intensity in most organizations, time away from work for several contiguous months will become common. Two-career couples will be able to enjoy this financial luxury, but one difference from the past is that instead of the organization's granting sabbaticals, independent contractors will program time off into their own career schedules.

The worker's agent. A new career will emerge—that of the worker's agent. Many people are knowledgeable in their areas of specialization but not good at selling themselves. Representatives will negotiate work contracts for them in return for a percentage of the workers' compensation received on a particular project. The role will resemble that of temporary agents so prevalent today, but it will involve much more complex negotiations. Worker agents will seek contracts covering the following: hiring bonuses, performance bonuses, regular project pay, sabbaticals, sick and disability pay, life insurance, guaranteed pay if the project is discontinued, and living expenses and transportation costs while working away from home. If the project is transacted online and the worker telecommutes, the agent may ask for the use of specific equipment for the duration of the project. Only the imagination can limit the options available in these negotiations.

Ensuring Organizational and Worker Security

Because of time allocations for a project, workers may have multiple projects in process simultaneously with more than one company.

Leaders are to be cautioned about possible implications of this arrangement—especially if workers are simultaneously working with competitors. Because corporate espionage is rising, background checks must be as thorough as legally possible so that organizational secrets will not be stolen.

New work arrangements also hold more security risks for workers. With many companies with very little or no track record starting up, workers or their agents should be careful to check out these new companies. Make certain that the organization is in a legitimate market, is forthright with the Internal Revenue Service, and has leaders with excellent reputations for honesty and integrity.

Ensuring an Adequate Labor Supply

Work-study programs. Another new work arrangement is the employment of Generation Y teens for part-time, high-tech jobs. This generation is computer literate and already has a role in the marketplace. Work-study programs are in place to retain these workers after they finish college. This arrangement is not new as work-study programs have been around for decades for college students. Now, however, organizations are reaching into high school for high-tech expertise because skilled workers are in such short supply.

Training. A paradox exists in the organization. Just as companies are shifting more career responsibility to workers, organizations are increasing the number of hours spent training them. Because of work complexity, uniqueness of projects, and constant turnover, training is an ongoing process. Because there is more work than there are skilled workers, organizations are choosing to instill worker skills through training. Some organizations are even furnishing cars to people who are low skilled and have previously been on welfare so they can drive to work, receive corporate training, and then be put on the job.

Training, however, is often incorporated into the work itself. Such companies as EDS and MCI do a majority of their training via computer intranets. The days of classroom stand-up lectures are diminishing. Generation Xers and Yers are astute at state-of-the-art training methodologies and prefer them, so training and work are often integrated.

Outsourcing. Outsourcing companies, which contract work from organizations, employ workers for specific functions. Organizations in turn stick to their core competencies—what they do best—and then contract out the rest of the work. Outsourcing companies today do everything from public relations, data processing, and accounting to mailing and maintenance. A new area for outsourcing is in e-commerce. For instance, if I order a gift online, that order is probably filled by an outsourcing company somewhere else. Because e-commerce is thriving, outsourcing firms for various e-commerce activities will also boom.

Work methods are increasingly creative. The new workforce profile lends itself well to new ways work will be structured. These new arrangements will mutually benefit both the worker and the organization.

 LEADERSHIP STRATEGIES

✓ Survey the demographics of your workplace. Include gender, ethnicity, household types, and dominant generations.

✓ Design work processes, compensation packages, reward systems, and work assignments to match the values of the demographic mix from the above study.

✓ Assess the new design that you implemented from the above strategy for productivity improvement.

✓ Design security measures to check backgrounds of contract workers and to ensure that these workers do not transfer company secrets to other enterprises.

✓ Become astute at negotiating with worker agents resulting in a win-win situation for the worker and the organization.

✓ Install a program for recruiting young high school or college computer-literate people who can join your organization in a work-study program. This will offer opportunities for potential employees for the organization and take advantage of available young talent.

QUESTIONS FOR CONTEMPLATION

1. What is the workforce composition of your organization?

2. How do you expect it to change over the next ten years?

3. Has your organization adapted work, benefits, extra services, and organizational culture to the changing behaviors and values?

4. Which generation's values dominate your organizational culture?

5. How will your organizational culture need to change to reflect new generational values in the next three to five years?

6. How will your organization adapt to new values and behaviors without alienating present generations?

7. Do you have a plan to carry out your answers to questions 5 and 6 above?

8. How might your organization employ creative ways of structuring work?

ENDNOTES

1. Families and Work Institute, New York, New York, *1997 National Study of the Changing Workforce.*

2. Ibid.

3. Kiplinger Washington Editors, *Kiplinger Washington Letter,* 23 December 1997 (Washington, D.C.). By permission of the Kiplinger Editor.

4. Tom Brokaw, *The Greatest Generation* (New York: Random House, 1998).

CHAPTER 8

The Successful 21st Century Worker

QUALITIES LEADERS SEEK IN WORKERS

I conducted a retreat for high-level leaders from such major global companies as Northwestern Mutual Life Insurance Company, J. C. Penney International, and Rauscher, Pierce, Refsnes. One of the goals of that retreat was to discern the three major qualities those leaders look for in recruiting people for the 21st century. In no special rank order, these qualities are:

- How to think
- How to relate
- How to use appropriate productive technology

No doubt, knowledge workers will dominate the 21st century workforce. As I defined in Chapter 1, knowledge workers are workers who earn their living by analyzing, managing, and making judgments based on knowledge extracted from information. Even though some of them may never lead anyone else, they will at least be required to lead themselves. They must be self-governing and to a great extent self-organizing, so it follows that leaders put the three skills listed above at the top of their lists.

How to Think

For many years most people were told what to think. From kindergarten on, students were asked to sit in the same seat daily, memorize facts, stand in straight lines, and color houses they drew in either white or light brown. I remember a creative fellow student in second grade coloring his house bright blue—he got an F in art for being unrealistic.

Memorization is not enough anymore. The environment is changing so rapidly that many memorized rules may be obsolete by college graduation. Even if the facts are still true, many new problems must be solved. Employers want workers who can solve problems both independently and as part of a group. There may not always be a structured formula to follow or an expert to ask. Just the same, the problem must be solved.

In summary, 21st century workers must be problem solvers and make decisions by using complex reasoning skills.

How to Relate

People skills are unusually important in this new millennium. People skills were once termed *soft skills,* relegating them to second place behind the *hard skills* that deal with technology and task-related skills. No more. People skills are just as important as hard skills in the 21st century. With continued mergers and acquisitions, people must learn to cooperate to produce positive results. Teamwork is necessary for organizational success. Without cooperation and positive relationships, teams don't have a chance of being effective.

In Chapter 7, I discussed the diversity that will exist in the workplace. Without a concerted effort to establish good relationships, diversity initiatives will fail. More than ever, we must all work together in unity to accomplish lofty goals; and good interpersonal relationships are a necessary ingredient to achieving goals. (I'll take a more in-depth look at interpersonal intelligence in Chapter 10.)

How to Use Appropriate Productive Technology

Everyone must be computer literate. I know some leaders who proclaim, "I don't want anything to do with computers. I don't even want one on my desk. My secretary can handle anything on the computer that I need." That is not a cutting-edge attitude. *Everyone should be able to use basic communication techniques and company software packages.*

I recently worked with a government agency where 50 percent of the employees had no clue how to use the Internet, and approximately 33 percent didn't use a personal computer—a spot far behind the technology curve. Leaders in this government agency are not getting maximum organizational performance because of the lack of proper technology usage. Worker productivity is suffering, workers are on their way to obsolescence, and leadership ability is being questioned.

These three skills—thinking, relating, and using technology—will divide the haves from the have nots in the future. Those who don't possess these skills will be at a great disadvantage in the new economy, whereas those who are expert at these skills will be amply rewarded. One of these skills alone is not enough to get ahead; it takes all three. Great leaders recognize this and keep these qualities in mind when hiring.

ATTRIBUTES THAT ENHANCE WORKER PERFORMANCE

There are nine important attributes, in addition to the three skills described above, that enhance worker performance:

1. Flexibility
2. Wisdom
3. Project orientation
4. Pursuit of continuous learning
5. Self-reliance
6. Self-motivation
7. Emphasis on core competencies
8. Risk orientation
9. Interdependence

Flexibility

To be successful, workers must be open to change and stand ready to reinvent themselves at a moment's notice. If change is a system's reaction to disequilibrium, then we can make the assumption that work will rarely be in a state of complete balance. People who are uncomfortable working in this kind of atmosphere will find the 21st century very unsettling. Embracing rather than resisting rapid change typically holds workers in good stead.

I have always been taught that the oak is the strongest of all trees, and powerful leaders have been compared to mighty oaks. I learned something while watching the video, *Texas*, based on James Michener's novel by the same name. Michener claimed that the willow is stronger than the oak tree because it is more flexible.[1] Its branches are agile and supple, blowing with the wind, not against it. They flow rather than resist. In recalling Charles Darwin's theory of evolution, we speak of the survival of the fittest, the fittest to Darwin being "the most flexible and adaptable."[2]

Wisdom

Wisdom is often associated with age. The problem here lies in the belief that younger people cannot have wisdom. The assumption is that wisdom comes with experience, which accumulates as people get older.

Let me offer another definition of wisdom: *Wisdom is knowledge plus vision.* With the old definition of wisdom, we see backwards. In times of slow change, that works. During rapid change, that type of wisdom has limited usefulness. With my definition of wisdom, we look forward, and anyone can possess that type of wisdom. Wisdom then becomes the sum of what you know and your ability to look ahead with clarity. I believe that what you know determines what you see, and what you see determines what you will accomplish.

In my consulting practice, I am blessed with opportunities to travel all over the country and meet people from every socioeconomic level. In one particular state, I was working with a school system on implementing changes necessary to equip students with skills for success in the 21st century. I met children who had never traveled more than 60 miles from home and whose perspective of the world was different from that of the children who had visited other states.

First, the nontravelers envisioned danger, believing that the world is a frightening, violent place because their knowledge was limited to what they saw on television. Second, they had no desire to travel much beyond their 60-mile limit because they were afraid to explore the outside world.

These children, if not encouraged to move beyond their imposed limitations, will always have a small amount of wisdom resulting in a skewed view of the world. Their reality consists of so little true knowledge that they are restricting their lives. What they know—or do not know—determines their view of the world and will then determine their destiny.

I believe that astute young people can have wisdom, a 21st century workplace requirement. Workers need it—leaders must have it.

How does one acquire wisdom? Here are some suggestions:

- Become acquainted with all necessary information resources.
- Read everything possible pertaining to your profession and your areas of interest.
- Daydream about the future. Start connecting events. Ask *what if* questions. For example, what if computers became so smart that they could do my work? Or, what if all the automobiles in the world were powered by solar energy? What industries would be affected? How would that affect my life?
- Form groups to use collective wisdom and brainstorm these *what ifs* together.
- Determine the probability of these *what ifs* happening.
- Discuss practical plans for eventualities.

In acquiring wisdom, it is difficult to determine which comes first—knowledge or vision. To see ahead with clarity, you need specific knowledge. However, to determine the information you need and convert it to knowledge, you need to have a focused vision. Knowledge and vision must coexist to produce wisdom.

Project Orientation

Projects by definition are temporary. They have a beginning and an end. Effective new millennium workers must be committed to the temporary. Projects will develop around problems that need to be solved. Whether designing a new automobile or reengineering a department, people will assemble, maybe even virtually, to solve the problem and then move on. Workers will advance from project to project within and outside the organization.

Together the project members will define desired outcomes or deliverables according to organizational specifications and will then self-organize in ways that maximize each person's expertise. Normally, additional project goals are speed and accuracy, so workers who thrive in temporary projects will fare well in the new economy. Project-oriented people must learn to establish relationships quickly, change mind-sets often, and be astute at adapting to interactive teamwork.

Pursuit of Continuous Learning

Every experience offers a learning opportunity. Smart 21st century workers will always ask themselves: What did I learn from this experience? Even mistakes can be learning opportunities. Wise workers will communicate their learning experiences to others, so it is hoped that the organization has created an avenue for this communication to take place.

Individuals must continually educate themselves to keep up with state-of-the-art technology and methodology. The responsibility for lifelong learning rests solely on the worker. Organizations may provide training, but smart workers don't depend on that. They aggressively seek out classes and experiences that will maintain their employability.

Self-Reliance

Careers lie within people—not within organizations. People create their own value; the organization does not create value for them. Self-reliance is synonymous with self-governance as a worker characteristic. Not only must people be career self-reliant, but they must also be independent of their organization financially and emotionally. They are really self-employed at all times and should run their life like a small business.

The paternalistic organization creates an attitude of dependency—a hypocritical paradigm. Not one organization in existence can guarantee an employee's future with that organization. Employees are responsible for securing their own future. Some workers are fortunate that their organizations have career centers to help them identify skills they need to hone and to help them assess their marketable skills. These centers suggest training opportunities that will be helpful to employees who will then find time to attend learning sessions, where different levels of help are available.

Some organizations announce changes that will take place and post the requirements for the changed employment. Most companies offer to pay for the training necessary to meet these requirements, although they may expect employees to schedule the training classes on their own time. It then becomes the employee's choice whether to stay with the company.

Emotional self-reliance is also a critical issue. No longer can workers depend on a boss to tell them what to do or a company that provides them with a feeling of psychological security. Because much of a worker's identity comes from the organization, the worker likes working for a successful company because it builds self-esteem. However, it is unhealthy for workers to allow their emotions to rise and fall with the ups and downs of the organization.

In addition to emotional self-reliance, workers should be financially self-reliant. They should have a financial plan that allows for career downtime. Older workers might become financially self-reliant through savings and investments. Younger workers often offset their risk by becoming part of a dual career couple, and it is hoped the planning is such that the family can live on one income for six to nine months. Also, each member of a dual career couple should work for different organizations in order to spread the risk of simultaneous downsizings.

Great leaders recognize the need to help workers become more self-reliant. They structure the organization in a way that fosters worker independence and move away from paternalistic relationships with workers. They state their requirements, create an atmosphere that invites stellar employees to work there, and then reward them for performing to expectations.

I spent a great portion of my book *Strategies 2000* addressing the need to be self-reliant. In 1986, when that book was written, it was evident that people needed to conduct their life as Me, Inc. In *Conquering Corporate Codependence*, I offered readers the skills necessary for exercising self-governance.[3] If a worker is dependent on the organization that is in turn dependent on the marketplace, then that worker is by definition codependent. It is when one breaks the cycle of organizational codependency that he or she can become self-reliant.

Self-Motivation

Even though we could assume that self-reliant individuals are also self-motivated, I have chosen to address self-motivation separately because it is possible for someone to be self-reliant and not self-motivated. Self-motivation indicates that one is moving toward a goal, executing properly and focused. A truly self-motivated person does not drift off course. That person commits, then delivers.

Emphasis on Core Competencies

Organizations and people see the need to focus on core competencies—what they do best. More than ever before, it is important to identify a specialty and work to strengthen it.

Workers often hear mixed messages. First, they are told they must be cross-functional so they can cover for others on their team if necessary. They do not have a rigid job description but must be able to work more broadly. On the other hand, workers are told that they must be very good at something. They must probe a specialty until they are expert at it. Then, if that expertise becomes obsolete, they must be acquainted with their transferable skills in order to move to another field of expertise. For example, a person may be skilled at finding information, analyzing it, then assimilating it into practical knowledge. Those skills are basic to becoming a librarian, a lawyer, a medical researcher, or a computer programmer. With proper education and acquisition of content expertise, one can move comfortably from one profession to another.

So, which is it, generalization or specialization? The answer: both. All of us must be great at something that is marketable. That something is the expertise that must be cultivated to excellence. Secondarily, we must be able to learn other skills to a lesser degree so that we can pinch hit for others on the team. Specific processes such as interviewing, budgeting, training, or recruiting can be learned and practiced cross-functionally. However, each team member must be better than anyone else in a particular field of expertise. For example, a design team is composed of experts in engineering, sales, marketing, and customer service. Although everyone can learn some processes, each member has a specialty, and no other team member can execute that specialty as well as the one who "owns" it.

Risk Orientation

The 21st century workplace is not for those who are risk reluctant or fainthearted. Try to calculate your risks before acting, although that may be impossible. Leaders as well as workers are increasingly being asked to make decisions based on faith, not on tangible evidence, especially in the new Internet industry. Leaders create a vision of their future, launch an Internet company, convince investors, recruit people—then go for it. Hard figures are lacking—only a lot of enthusiasm and the founder's best guess coupled with hope that the projections will come true. Today's environment rewards those willing to risk and win—but can punish those who risk and fail. So this is a time when courage must prevail and fear must take a back seat.

Risk-oriented individuals know that failure is not fatal. They can fail many times and still come out winners. The very first speech I ever delivered commercially was entitled *Give Yourself Permission to Win*. I spoke deeply from my heart. One day in the middle of my speech, I realized that to give yourself permission to win, you must first give yourself permission to fail. Unless you are not afraid to visibly fail and have people know about it, you will never experience big wins.

Interdependence

Because you are self-reliant and self-motivated doesn't mean that you can't be interdependent—a team player. The new millennium worker will be individually strong and collectively collaborative.

Fort Worth, Texas, is home to a wonderful Southwestern Exposition Rodeo each year. As a child, I remember being fascinated by the powerful, big, and beautiful Clydesdale horses pulling a stagecoach. A life lesson I learned from the rodeo announcer when he was describing the power of these horses was that one Clydesdale could pull a heavy load, but eight working together could pull hundreds of times more than any one horse working alone. I remember being puzzled at that, because even at a young age I could do the arithmetic.

I leaned over, tugged on my dad's arm, and asked, "Dad, if one horse can pull a load, wouldn't eight horses pull eight times that load? Why can eight horses pull hundreds of times more?" Dad answered with a statement I'll never forget. "Carolyn," he said, "it's the power of teamwork."

The power of teamwork remains true today. Multiple people working in unity are so much more powerful than the same number of people working independently.

LEADING THE SELF-GOVERNING WORKER

Human resources experts have for decades declared that only about 10 percent of the population is capable of entrepreneurship. Suddenly, organizations are asking almost every worker—especially knowledge workers—to be entrepreneurial, thus posing a huge dilemma. Finding people with needed skills as discussed above is difficult. Therefore, organizations may be forced to train workers to help them acquire these skills. Formal training activities can help, but the most valuable training comes from working repeatedly in an entrepreneurial environment. Knowledge workers are required to be self-governing.

Leading knowledge workers is a new science and an art. Very few organizations have a solid, knowledge worker leadership philosophy in place. Knowledge workers exchange what they know for compensation. Normally, they have several years of education beyond high school, with many holding doctoral degrees. They continually update their expertise through education and learning experiences from personal research and development. Knowledge workers exist in all professions: scientists, nurses, lawyers, software programmers, college professors, engineers, and physicians.

There is a difference between leading knowledge workers and managing knowledge. Some leaders think the two activities are the same, but that is just not true. Leading knowledge workers involves leading people, whereas managing knowledge involves planning, organizing, directing, and controlling systems and resources. In this section, I discuss the people portion of the equation.

I have spent a great deal of time over the past three decades working with knowledge workers, who have existed since the beginning of recorded history. What is novel is that knowledge workers make up about one-third of all workers, and the numbers will continue to grow until knowledge workers will dominate the workplace. In new dynamic industries such as telecommunications and the Internet, they already outnumber nonknowledge workers. Leaders must know certain general traits of knowledge workers in order to interact with them effectively. Let's examine those next. I've drawn my conclusions from three sources: personal work with knowledge workers, extensive literature surveys, and self-introspection as I myself am a knowledge worker.

General Traits of Knowledge Workers

These workers are specialists in their professions, have unique expertise, and like to examine their professional discipline with the goal of learning more. In their particular area, knowledge workers are very self-confident. Ideas are their commerce. Making a difference by applying their ideas or having the organization adopt them on a broad scale creates intrinsic reward.

Knowledge workers have been accused of being arrogant by outsiders. They like their area of practice so well that many feel that all other disciplines take second place to theirs. Preferring to associate and exchange knowledge with their peers, these workers are rather tribalistic. In their own subcultures, they have a language all their own and can be very critical of outsiders who don't know as much about their field as they do. Problems can arise because organizational leaders are usually considered outsiders. In the estimation of knowledge workers, nothing is worse than an incompetent person claiming to belong to their profession. That person is immediately rejected.

Knowledge workers set up turf with definite boundaries and are willing to go to war with other areas to protect the resources that feed their knowledge base. Be careful not to invade their turf—you'll be ejected. Recognition, especially by peers they respect, for their accomplishments is important to them. More than money, knowledge workers want to be complimented on an innovative idea or a job well done. Work itself is both a learning ground and reward system.

Because their work is so important to them, knowledge workers can become very narrowly focused, at times even forgetting the customer. They get involved in solving problems and sometimes don't remember such customer expectations as fast turnaround time or ease of application. Some knowledge workers try to override customer requests by forcing what they feel is best for the customer, even if the customer doesn't want what they offer.

Unless knowledge workers are stimulating change themselves, change is not their friend. Uncertainty is disconcerting to them. They create their own world in which they feel most comfortable and where variables are predictable.

Being told how to execute a task is unthinkable. Knowledge workers like to discover their own avenues for project delivery because they believe they know best. They bristle at command and control leadership. In their minds they are as good in their field as leaders are in theirs.

Knowledge workers would rather work with tasks than with people unless their specialty is leading people. If not, the day-to-day people challenges that leadership brings are considered energy and time wasters. Knowledge workers don't want to work for people and don't want people to work for them. They like to work with competent peers because exchanging knowledge with peers is exhilarating and creates the workers' energy.

Suggestions for Leadership

Finding and training knowledge workers. Knowledge workers are at a premium, so finding and retaining them is a real challenge. Besides the obvious traditional and online ways of recruiting, referrals are helpful. Good employees know the capabilities of colleagues and can often help entice them. When you are able to find and hire workers who are strong in their field, paying them well will help you keep them, although money is rarely the primary retention tool.

As a result of a labor shortage of knowledge workers, some organizations are partnering with high schools, universities, and community colleges with work-study programs. Students are hired to work part-time and in summers during high school, while attending community colleges or even while going to four-year colleges. College expenses are then paid by the company with the agreement that students will work for that company for a negotiated period of time after graduation. Partnerships with technology schools work in a similar fashion. All of these programs are having a resurgence today, even though they have been ongoing in engineering and high technology for the past 40 years. It is because of the tremendous shortage of knowledge workers today that work-study programs are becoming more formalized and purposeful.

It is also common practice to recruit and train college graduates in a rigorous training program. Some make it, some don't. Initial work assignments require long hours; trainees, in fact, may go for days with little or no sleep. Medical internships are known traditionally for sleepless nights and intensive work, an experiential model being used extensively in accounting and consulting firms as well as in high-tech companies.

Retaining knowledge workers. Organizations are getting really creative in methods of employee retention. One organization leases upscale automobiles for its employees, claiming that it is less expensive than employee turnover. Other organizations have common areas set up like family rooms where workers can take time off to play computer games, relax, or even sleep.

Knowledge workers are more productive when they set mutual goals with organizational leaders. The tougher the goal, the greater the challenge to knowledge workers. They enjoy solving challenging problems or stretching to reach their goals; the feeling of accomplishment is exhilarating. In project work, either the leader assembles a problem-solving team or the leader can choose a knowledge worker to build his or her own team. In empowered organizations, knowledge workers discover a problem, assemble an ad hoc team to fix it, and then report the results without the necessity of submitting to bureaucratic procedures.

It is important for leaders to stay tuned to knowledge workers' resource needs. Among other things, knowledge workers enjoy direct access to powerful, resourceful people as well as to necessary problem-solving technology. Teams should be allowed to self-organize and self-direct themselves to the greatest extent possible. However, measurements of progress or checkpoints must be built in to keep the team on the right track. Leaders and team members should mutually agree on types of checkpoints that are helpful. The leader should also be available to aid in correcting the direction when the team gets off track.

Great leaders emphasize knowledge sharing and, in fact, structure work to require sharing. Because knowledge workers consider their knowledge to be proprietary, however, they don't like to share what they consider to be theirs. Unless they are forced to share by the work environment, knowledge management is not workable.

Getting the most from knowledge workers. One of the leader's major challenges is how to multiply the production capabilities of knowledge workers. Alone, they can only produce a finite amount of work. They are only human and have only 24 hours a day. They get tired and productivity lags—an expensive arrangement. One way to get the most productivity from knowledge workers is to hire assistants for them. Lawyers use paralegals. Doctors have nurses. Consulting firms have paraprofessionals and use lots of trainees. Work becomes a training resource.

Another way to increase productivity is through good information management. A beginning insurance agent, for instance, can have all sorts of high-level information available from a database. The new agent might not yet have the expertise to project annuity payments for 30 years or exact death payments with dividends falling back into the cash value for 20 years. But software programs can do this. A competitor's policy can be compared immediately to the one the agent is offering the client. A sale can be consummated quickly because such information is readily available. The more information that is shared, the greater the productivity of knowledge workers.

Five Needs of Knowledge Workers

Great leaders understand and provide five needs to knowledge workers.

1. Knowledge. Knowledge workers need access to people for gathering information. Publish a reference list or a sort of yellow pages of expertise so knowledge workers can have information handy. State-of-the-art technology is also necessary for information retrieval. Such technologies as video conferencing, chat rooms, databases, shared white boards, interactive e-mail, pagers, the Internet, intranets, and telephones are necessary technology for knowledge workers' productivity.

2. Vision. Great leaders work with knowledge workers on a big picture organizational vision. Leaders receive input from knowledge workers to design a project's vision and then mutually picture the project's deliverables. Knowledge workers prefer to participate in the construction of the project's vision.

3. Hope. To reach their goals, knowledge workers must believe that their goals can be reached. In other words, they must have hope and believe that it can be done. One of the most influential ways to instill hope in people is to use storytelling as a motivational technique. Throughout history, stories have been inspirational and have

been handed down from generation to generation. Now, the introduction of the story into the workplace is gaining momentum. People
enjoy hearing stories; they have a beginning, an end, and are able to
make specific points metaphorically. It's a great idea to have several
stories available that will fit the situation at hand. For instance, if the
project is really tough and the deadline rapidly approaching, leaders
might tell a story of a past experience in which people overcame great
odds to meet a deadline. The story would emphasize the tremendous
rewards that were reaped and the great impact the experience had on
both the organization and the customer.

4. Harmony. People in general want balance, and problems
typically create imbalance. Individuals will therefore work hard to
solve problems in an attempt to reinstate systemic balance. A problem's solution is a motivational technique in and of itself. The best
way to produce harmony is to join together in teams people with complementary expertise and complementary personalities. The objective
of the overall project, which unifies the team, is more important than
any person or idea in the project. Each person executes his or her own
task with the aim of achieving the overall goal of the project.

5. Sense of control. Knowledge workers are uncomfortable if
they feel out of control. They want to be in charge of their own destiny, so make certain they have well-defined goals, measures, and feedback checkpoints aligned with predefined avenues for correction. If
a problem comes up and no predefined avenue for correction is available, then leaders must work with team members to find a solution.

Peak Performance Inhibitors

Even though organizations are moving toward new models at a
rapid pace, many organizational cultures are lagging behind. People
typically try to sabotage the change process if possible, although the
effort is mostly unconscious and designed to be self-protective. Nevertheless, measures to sabotage change inhibit workers' peak performance and decrease organizational productivity. Great leaders have
the courage to confront saboteurs and work with them in an attempt
to move them to peak performance. If such efforts are not effective
after a short period, then the resistant workers will be downsized
because the organization cannot afford to keep them on the payroll.

There are four inhibitors to workers achieving peak performance as discussed below.

1. Feelings of employment entitlement. Some workers feel they are entitled to stay with a company just because they have been there a long time. Sometimes their performance decreases, and they no longer try as hard as they once did, feeling they have earned the right to slack off. Such an attitude costs the company money, so organizations can no longer afford to pay a worker top wages for less than stellar performance.

2. Refusing to share information. Some workers refuse to be a team player, failing to share information and seeking only individual recognition and reward. When a worker withholds information, the whole organization suffers. Companies are reporting millions of dollars in savings from the implementation of information-sharing technology, so it is imperative that workers are willing to share. Refusing penalizes productivity.

3. Inability to handle workplace insecurity. Many leaders expect dedication, passion, and on-call availability 24 hours a day from workers without guaranteeing them future employment. Because of workplace competition, workers often don't admit their plight. Instead, they exhibit physical symptoms, such as chest pains or backaches, which they deny even to themselves. When workers refuse to acknowledge personal needs and remain in denial, problems can increase in seriousness. Such emotional symptoms as depression or anxiety rob workers of the ability to perform at their peak.

4. Seeking individual attention at team expense. Because they feel insecure, some workers attempt heroic deeds to make themselves indispensable to the organization. They need the attention gained from solving problems or working longer hours than anyone else. They pull political maneuvers to endear themselves to key people in the organization and are driven to overwork. Such behavior alienates fellow team members. Rather than work toward team unity, the attention-getters want all the credit for achievement to go to them, slowing team momentum and causing productivity to suffer.

LEADERSHIP STRATEGIES

✓ Make certain that you as a leader have the necessary worker qualities listed in this chapter. It is impossible to be a great leader and good example to workers in the 21st century without these characteristics.

✓ If you are lacking in any of these qualities, initiate a personal development program for yourself so you can acquire them.

✓ Make a checklist of characteristics you look for when recruiting a new worker. Compare this list with the necessary worker qualities mentioned in this chapter. Assess whether the applicants have enough of these qualities to be successful in the 21st century workplace.

✓ Assign a human resources professional or hire a consultant to develop a system for your organization that will measure workers' thinking and relational abilities as well as their technological literacy and the nine other qualities that enhance worker performance.

✓ Install an organizational program to overcome worker deficiencies indicated from the above assessment.

✓ Implement a special training program for teaching leaders how to manage knowledge workers.

✓ Because knowledge workers have a great deal of power in the workplace, leading them with effectiveness will enhance the bottom line. Devise ways of measuring knowledge workers' contribution to the bottom line.

✓ Measure variances in bottom-line performance with the introduction of new leadership techniques for knowledge workers.

✓ Identify people that are exhibiting peak performance inhibitors. Because such behavior can be the source of organizational politics and worker polarization, it is important to design and conduct interventions to avoid allowing workers to inhibit peak performance.

QUESTIONS FOR CONTEMPLATION

1. In what ways is your organization preparing people for the top three 21st century workplace skills: how to think; how to relate; how to use appropriate productive technology?

2. Has your organization developed methods for measuring the nine other attributes that enhance worker performance?

3. What special techniques might your organizational leaders implement to more effectively lead knowledge workers?

4. In general, which knowledge worker traits discussed in this chapter describe your key knowledge workers?

5. How is your organization providing for the five needs of knowledge workers mentioned in the latter part of this chapter?

6. Have you noted any of the four peak performance inhibitors being exhibited in your organization? If so, which ones? How are they being addressed?

ENDNOTES

1. James A. Michener, *Texas* (New York: Random House, 1985).

2. Darwin's definition of survival is quoted in Norman R. Augustine's "Reshaping an Industry: Lockheed Martin's Survival Story," *Harvard Business Review* (May-June, 1997): 83.

3. Carolyn Corbin with Gene Busnar, *Conquering Corporate Codependence: Lifeskills for Making It Within or Without the Corporation* (Englewood Cliffs, New Jersey: Prentice-Hall, 1993).

CHAPTER 9

Merging Organizational Strategies

One of the prominent keys to successful new century leadership is the recognition that all organizations are more similar than they are different. This is true even though there are technical differences between for-profit and nonprofit enterprises, governments are run differently than religious institutions, and the operating goals of schools are dissimilar to those of businesses. Great leaders know that qualities of all organizations are being combined in unique ways to forge a blended type of enterprise. In the blending of organizational models, dynamic and innovative new enterprises are born.

CURRENT ORGANIZATIONAL MODELS

In this chapter, I describe the prominent models of organizations today and then provide examples of the mixing of these models. Let's first look at some common characteristics of these paradigms, which I have separated into eight categories: for-profits, nonprofits, universities, religious institutions, governments, the military, sports teams, and entertainment enterprises.

For-Profits

For-profit corporations are designed to produce a profit while executing their mission. This involves careful cost containment and good stewardship of a company's funds for the owners—that is, the shareholders. Customer satisfaction is of utmost importance, and ultimately the customer decides whether the business survives. Workers are paid to perform tasks, and rewards to all workers, including leaders, are ultimately based on company and individual performance.

Nonprofits

Historically, nonprofit organizations have not been as conscious of cost containment as for-profit organizations. These enterprises may be politically driven because it is such stakeholders as boards of trustees and donors that decide the organizational mission. These outside forces have a great deal of managerial power. The mission is cause oriented, and workers, both paid and voluntary, are motivated by a passion for the mission. Some organizations resemble for-profits in the work they accomplish; for example, some training organizations are nonprofit while others, which offer similar services, are profit driven.

Universities

Universities are designed to provide education and innovation, and until now, they have been the primary employers of knowledge workers. The customer is the student or end user of the innovation discovered at the university. However, like many nonprofits, universities can be politically driven by outside stakeholders such as a board of regents and benefactors for private institutions or the legislature and taxpayers for public institutions.

Religious Institutions

Religious institutions have differing forms of governing bodies depending on the particular religious affiliation or denomination represented. Generally, their goal is to transform lives and support the spiritual growth of their members. Most of the work of these organizations is performed by volunteers driven by a passion for their mission, which is based on their faith. Their customer ultimately is the Power they worship. In most cases, that Power is God, whom members of the organization serve by serving people. The terms *evangelical, zeal, passion, mission, spirituality,* and *faith* were first used in reference to the goals of religious institutions. These organizations can also be politically motivated. Many are largely governed by people outside the paid staff.

Governments

Democratic governments, whose major goal is to provide public services, are unique. Their owners and customers can be the same people, for taxpayers (the people) own governments. Most of the people democratic governments serve pay taxes. Profits are not their concern, although responsible stewardship of taxpayer money is highly recommended.

The Military

The military model with its emphasis on rank has been in existence for thousands of years. There are leaders and there are the followers who unquestioningly follow the leaders. Rules, structure, and strictly enforced discipline characterize the military model. One of the major jobs of leaders is to motivate the followers (the troops) to buy into the mission to the point that they would be willing to die for the organization's cause. History records great military leaders who have exhibited heroic strength, wisdom, courage, character, and charisma, but history also records many cruel military leaders. In both cases, however, the leaders were able to find followers willing to make great personal sacrifices to accomplish their mission.

Sports Teams

The sports model is characterized by a coach and players exhibiting coordinated teamwork. Each member of a sports organization has a distinct set of skills and works in unison with the other team players to accomplish a specific goal. The coach's job is to help group members hone their skills and be the best that they can be. The coaching goal is to orchestrate the diverse skills of each player into a unified winning team.

Entertainment Enterprises

The entertainment model is characterized by temporary projects, as very few entertainers are permanently employed. When a project is contracted, the director sets up the various character and administrative roles that people are to play. Projects are on an ad hoc basis—temporary with a beginning and an end. Because the success of a project is determined by customer ratings, it is imperative to develop an entertainment project with the consumer in mind.

BLENDING MODELS

In the first quarter of the fourth century A.D., the Roman government influenced how the Catholic Church was organized. After World War II, the corporate world adopted the command and control military model. The adaptation and blending of models is not a new phenomenon but has been occurring since the first millennium. Now, however, paradigm merging and blending are quickly becoming widespread. The best of each model is being used to create a paradigm that best serves a particular organization. Rather than just one 21st century model for business, for example, as some experts have espoused, there seem to be several alternatives. Great leaders choose an organizational paradigm that aligns with their mission and marketplace.

The remainder of this chapter shows how enterprises have successfully blended organizational models.

BLENDING A BUSINESS AND A NONPROFIT MODEL

Girl Scouts of the USA (GSUSA)

In the mid-1970s, the Girl Scout organization identified the need to coordinate long-range and short-term planning. "Before that time there was no integrated process from the council to the national organizational level," says Peggy Pruett, assistant national director for planning and administration. "It was difficult to meet goals without a system that would be useful at both the local and national levels."

Pruett continues:

> Our leaders were aware that technology would continue to create profound changes in the economy, the labor force, and the educational priorities of our country. With this knowledge as a basis for action, representatives of councils and the national organization came together to design a management system that continually examines internal and

external trends and their possible effect on girls, families, and the organization as a whole. The concept of a model for corporate planning in Girl Scouting was approved by the National Board in 1976 and installed as the national organization's planning and management system in early 1977. Great care has been taken to preserve the totality of the process as refinements and improvements have been instituted. For 20 years we have achieved amazing results from these management strategies.

That early vision and hard work paid off. GSUSA is now recognized as an outstanding organization and is a role model for leadership among all types of enterprises.

The Girl Scouts are a prime example of the blending of business and nonprofit models to produce an exemplary organization. "We took the best of business practices and managed in a businesslike way," explains Frances Hesselbein, chairman of the board of governors and editor-in-chief of the Peter F. Drucker Foundation for Nonprofit Management. Before joining the Drucker Foundation, Hesselbein was CEO of the GSUSA from 1976 to 1990. "Nonprofits have a common bottom line—that of changing lives. They are stewards of the public trust and public mores. We never violate that trust and always manage for the mission," she continues.

In 1976, the total membership of almost 3 million members was 95 percent white; and 650,000 men and women were volunteers with less than 1 percent employed staff. In partnership, the national organization and local councils tripled the racial and ethnic membership; and the number of volunteers now exceeds 1 million. Hesselbein was quick to state that great leaders know that they do not implement change alone. It takes an astute team of passionate, dedicated people to execute the mission. At a time when it was difficult to recruit volunteers and members of youth organizations, the Girl Scouts were thriving.

To turn the Girl Scouts into a growth-oriented organization, according to Hesselbein, the organization became mission focused, values based, and demographics driven. Hesselbein states:

> We formed focus groups to find out what our customers wanted—some of them children only five years old. We invested in good people and understood the tremendous power of volunteers mobilized around a few powerful goals.

We threw out the hierarchy and implemented the circular organization management systems. This model has three concentric circles with the CEO in the center, the CEO's direct reports in the next circle, and the people reporting to the CEO's reports in the outer ring. We were one great executive staff corps serving the movement. Our language and behavior were inclusive.

Hesselbein believes that the most important thing that nonprofit leaders can do to ensure their organization is successful is to focus on their mission. "The mission is their purpose," she states, "their reason for being. The mission statement should be short and powerful. Peter Drucker often tells people that the mission statement ought to fit on a T-shirt. People must be motivated to be faithful to that mission and to further that mission. And every three years an organization's leaders should revisit the mission and revise it if necessary."

Marsha Johnson Evans retired as an admiral from the U.S. Navy to accept the position of the national executive director of the Girl Scouts of the USA in January 1998. In Evan's words:

> The national board had identified a need to develop a consistent Girl Scout image much like companies use a brand image. So we began a substantial effort involving staff and people at both the national and local board levels to reframe who we are. We have had an excellent record throughout the years, but the public identified us by activities such as cookie sales, camping, and arts and crafts. Girl Scouting is so much more, and we needed the public, and the girls themselves, to understand this. So we all worked together to crystallize our image and capture what we feel passionate about—that Girl Scouting is where girls grow strong. Our goal is to be available to every girl everywhere. Our organization helps girls develop their full individual potential; relate to others with increasing understanding, skill, and respect; develop values to guide their actions and provide the foundation for sound decision making; and contribute to the improvement of society through their abilities, leadership skills, and cooperation with others.

Today there are 3.685 million Girl Scouts—2.7 million girl members and 860,000 adult members. Through membership in the World Association of Girl Guides and Girl Scouts, GSUSA is part of a worldwide family of 10 million girls and adults in 140 countries. Evans explains:

> One of our most critical issues is the need for more adult volunteers. More girls want to become Girl Scouts than we can accept. So we are constantly recruiting volunteer leaders. One of our current initiatives is to expand to communities along the Mexican border in Texas, New Mexico, and California. We are using English language instruction and bilingual materials designed to give all girls the same opportunities. My own navy background coupled with business initiatives has helped us design a unifying, motivating image and refine our focus. Girl Scouts is an organization on the move—anticipating needs. We are actively preparing leaders for the 21st century.[1]

After visiting with former and current leaders and researching various areas of the Girl Scouts, I can understand why the largest organization for girls and women in the world is also the best run. Thus, the Girl Scouts of the USA is a fine example of the organizational blending of a business and a nonprofit model that was accomplished without compromising the integrity of either paradigm.

BLENDING A UNIVERSITY AND A BUSINESS MODEL

Because a third or more of today's workers in business are knowledge workers, our research team decided to find a model that business could use as a pattern for designing ways to manage knowledge workers. We turned to the university because higher education has been managing and motivating its knowledge workers (professors, who are experts in their respective fields) for more than a century and have thus had considerable experience.

Arizona State University (ASU)

"We have learned how to bring knowledge workers on board and encourage them to grow and work together," says Janice Reeb, ASU's human resources coordinator, who oversees three universitywide programs: the Employee Orientation Program, the Leadership Development Program, and the Employee Recognition Program. According to Reeb:

> They [knowledge workers] must have a sense of their importance. Our orientation program—once just an explanation of the paperwork processes—is now a dynamic, interactive multimedia overview of the university. They find out about the resources available to them. We also provide a one-stop shopping opportunity where they can do everything from acquire forms to purchase season tickets to turn in completed paperwork.
>
> Our second program, the Leadership Development Program, is multitiered. We present a President's Breakfast series once a month for the one hundred highest-level university leaders. We have speakers such as the President of the Arizona Board of Regents, former Secretary of State Henry Kissinger, and U.S. Ambassador to the United Nations Jeanne Kirkpatrick. Considering global issues and trends enables our knowledge workers to expand their outlook and align themselves with this new vision.
>
> As part of the University's Employee Recognition Program, we hold an Employee Recognition Festival. The booths at the festival showcase how we contribute as an institution and in the community. This celebration of our mutual contribution is held during spring break so faculty and staff can attend with their families, and children can see what Mom and Dad do at work. In addition to luncheons for work anniversaries for both faculty and staff, there is the President's Medal for Teams. This is an award to recognize cross-functional teams made up of professors, operations people, and staff who have developed and implemented an award-winning project. One award-winning system was online registration, which had a positive impact on students and university personnel. Recognizing the value of individuals for their expertise and their daily involvement in excel-

lence is an imperative for managing today's knowledge worker. ASU's leadership reflects this mentality and respect for the value of the individual contributor.

We believe this type of focus has been instrumental in moving ASU rapidly forward as a national leader. Last year the university attracted 33 National Merit Scholarship students. This year the number of National Merit Scholarship students has grown to 142. So the leadership of faculty and staff and the quality of university programs has created an ethos throughout the institution and has increased our competitiveness nationally as well.

University of Southern California (USC)

Dr. David W. Stewart, deputy dean of faculty of the Marshall School of Business at USC, believes that business faculty members, like all professionals, are motivated by a complex array of factors. "In a research environment, such as ours, the opportunities for professional freedom, selection of work content and structure, and recognition by peers are the strongest motivators," claims Stewart. "Salary is a necessary part of our recognition system, but it is not the most important part of the system. Salaries must be commensurate with the market but, beyond this, play only a modest role in motivating faculty members. Similarly, tenure and job security are necessary to compete for the most talented faculty members, but are not primary motivators."

The Marshall School and the university offer a number of awards for outstanding work. Merit pay is based on a variety of sources ranging from student teaching evaluations to peer review of research. Although provided with guidelines, department heads exercise a great deal of freedom in managing and motivating the faculty. "We believe that markets work," Stewart asserts. "Competition among departments for resources and students is a healthy thing. The key is avoiding the creation of unfair advantages."

George Washington University (GWU)

Dr. Jeffrey Lenn, senior associate dean of the School of Business and Public Management at GWU contends that the school's main mission is to provide a context in which knowledge workers or faculty can achieve their goals. "Like any knowledge worker or professional," he claims, "being recognized as an accomplished professional is the most important issue to professors. There are a number of ways you can recognize them: recognition by colleagues both inside and outside the university as well as recognition by students."

Outstanding performance at GWU is recognized with an annual performance review, in which colleagues make the decision about each other's performance. Decisions are reviewed by the deans and central administration, and performance is then rewarded in a variety of ways, including salary increases, teaching awards presented annually based on student input, recognition in internal newsletters and external quarterly reports, promotion, and tenure. New at GWU is a program whereby those who have been recently promoted or tenured are asked to present a speech on their research and take part with the dean's office in a celebration. If the honorees prefer a less formal atmosphere, the dean's office will schedule a luncheon where honorees can discuss their career or their research in any manner they wish.

"The School of Business is going through change at GWU and wherever there is change, debates occur," Lenn states. "However, we stay focused on the strategic plan with a common mission statement, which cuts down on turf wars. But we do also have room for diversity."

Research conclusions. Common themes seem apparent in how these universities lead their knowledge workers. Although many of the same methods are found in business, they are already proven in the university and should be taken seriously as primary ways of motivating, rewarding, and retaining valuable workers. Common themes found in the university milieu are these:

- A major motivator for knowledge workers is recognition for accomplishments in their areas of expertise.
- Freedom in selecting how they work and what they work on is also a major motivator for knowledge workers.
- These workers accept evaluations best if input comes from peers and customers (in this case, students) with review and additional input by their leaders.
- To keep knowledge workers on track, they must buy in to the mission and the organization's strategic plan. In spite of competitive turf wars and freedom of work, the focus on mission and the strategic plan keeps knowledge workers on an acceptable timeline and motivates them to target common organizational goals.

BLENDING GOVERNMENT, CIVIC, BUSINESS, AND NONPROFIT MODELS

Center for Citizen Initiatives

The nonprofit Center for Citizen Initiatives (CCI) was founded in 1983 by Sharon Tennison, who has served as its CEO from the beginning. The San Francisco headquarters has a staff of 30 plus 7 CCI partner offices in Russia with 70 employees.

"Our philosophy is to learn what Russians want or need. We don't make the assumption that we know what's best for them," explains Tennison. "If they want help with alcoholism, as our Russian friends did in 1984, we helped them start the AA program in Russia. If they were tackling a pollution problem as in 1989, we supported their early environmental projects with information and funding. When they asked for help with agriculture, we transplanted the U.S. agricultural extension model to Russian soil. Russian entrepreneurs in 1989 requested CCI to provide business training."

The Center was the first to train Russians in how to grow companies and presently implements the largest business training program in the field for non–English-speaking Russian business managers.

"Russian women in 1993 requested CCI to help them with microapparel operations located in their apartments. We created RISE, the best-known apparel microbusiness incubator and loan program in Russia," states Tennison.

She remarks that people often ask her: "What are you doing developing business in Russia? You're a not-for-profit organization!" Her reply: "Russia needs to learn how to build businesses and make profits so the Russian citizens will be fed, their cities will have a tax base, and the country can finally join the free nations of the world! It's real simple."

CCI works with the U.S. State Department and members of Congress. It receives funding from USIA and USAID; and American foundations, philanthropists, and memberships provide additional funds. The Center's annual budget is about $5 million. In-kind contributions of about $2.5 million from Rotarians, Kiwanians, and Russian participants collectively share the approximately $1 million a year cost for training, bringing CCI's total annual budget to about $9 million.

"I've been thrilled to find that Russian businessmen and businesswomen have a deep social consciousness. CCI's 1999 statistics show that close to 80 percent of CCI-trained Russian entrepreneurs running small and medium-sized private businesses routinely make donations and in-kind contributions directly to disadvantaged Russian citizens. These include help for orphanages, kindergartens, and schools, rebuilding churches, and assorted other types of help to Russia's needy," Tennison points out. "The faster we help them get their businesses on their feet, the faster traditional types of nonprofit needs will be met in Russia."

About 10,000 businesspeople across the United States volunteer to sponsor Russian entrepreneurs through their Rotary and Kiwanis Clubs, setting up full training schedules in local companies and factories. Russian business owners have a chance to look at a range of healthy businesses in their industry sector. Company presidents, department heads, and CFOs conduct workshops and on-site training on how to grow their companies. "They tell us all their business secrets; it's amazing!" report Russians in every delegation.

Having Americans invest time in training Russians free of charge is enormous. Many Russians report: "I saw my future in those American companies." "In America I got my direction confirmed; without knowing it, I was going in the right direction." "If we had the conditions the Americans have, Russia could be the fastest-growing economy in the world!"

American businesspeople love this kind of volunteer activity. According to Tennison:

> It meets a need, albeit unconscious much of the time, which their everyday business lives do not provide. Giving of themselves, their experience, their business secrets, ends up adding value to their bottom line–oriented lives. Some of these civic clubs have signed up over and over to train an ever-growing list of Russian delegations coming to the United States to learn from them. The clubs' public relations committees frequently announce, "The Russians are coming!" Thank God, this time it's a wonderful, heart-warming meeting of people who, in former years, could have never dreamed this kind of opportunity would occur.
>
> There is no need for boundaries between nonprofits, for-profits, government, and education. It should all be one

large interlacing, interacting net that responds to citizens as needed. It is hard to predict whether CCI's exchange of business information and principles is in essence for profit or not for profit. After years of designing and overseeing this kind of training for Russians, I believe the nontangible, human assets gained on both sides are every bit as powerful as the tangible, hard-line business concepts—perhaps even more so.

BLENDING A RELIGIOUS MODEL WITH E-BUSINESS AND MARKETING

In the intense literature survey that we conducted for this book, I have witnessed on multiple occasions the use of words that were originally used in religious institutions and are now being used in the business world. For instance, many e-commerce companies claim they sell investors and potential employees on their ideas based on faith. Their leaders, they say, must lead with evangelical zeal. In the electronic world, risk is high, and stakeholders must have faith in things they cannot see.

In *Radical Marketing,* authors Sam Hill and Glenn Rifkin advocate the position that companies have a marketing department composed of *passionate missionaries.*[2] Today's business world can be compared to the first century's Christian church. In the beginning, there was only a small group of believers who had such passion for what they postulated that they were willing to risk their lives and personal fortunes to advocate their tenets. Their message, carried by missionaries, eventually became accepted globally by more than 25 percent of the world's population. The business arena, especially the electronic business world, is adopting a similar strategy as it pioneers new territory.

By having faith in their ideas and leading with passionate enthusiasm, these leaders aim to take their organizations into unexplored territory—and succeed.

ADAPTING BUSINESS SKILLS TO HIGHER EDUCATION

Jones International University (JIU)

Glenn R. Jones, a pioneer of the U.S. cable industry purchased his first cable television system in 1967. His company, Jones Intercable, grew to become one of the ten largest cable companies in the United States. "Our company and its affiliates have been involved with technology for more than 30 years. For nearly 13 years, we have been fusing this technology with education," says Jones. Jones's business expertise became the springboard for his creation of a number of innovative educational enterprises, which include Jones International University (JIU), Knowledge TV, JonesKnowledge.com, and Global Alliance for Transnational Education (GATE).

But higher education's online future received a major boost in March 1999 when JIU became the first academic institution operating wholly on the Internet to receive the same form of accreditation as traditional colleges and universities. Founded in 1995, JIU exists entirely in cyberspace. It is the first online university to receive accreditation from the North Central Association of Colleges and Schools, a nationally recognized accrediting body. The university combines technology with educational content to offer degree and certificate programs to students around the world. The virtual classroom environment also provides more flexibility to students who may not be able to attend classes at a bricks-and-mortar college campus because of geographic distances or work schedules and personal commitments. A survey conducted for JIU found that 70 percent of Americans said they have considered taking a class or course of study to help further their career or pursue a skill or topic of interest. But in today's fast-paced world, not being able to take time out for traditional classroom learning can be a barrier to getting ahead.

Committed to the development of barrier-free education for adult learners in the information age, JIU fulfills the school motto, "Wherever you are, we are." JIU, a private, for-profit university, offers 18 certificate programs, a bachelor's completion degree, and a master's degree in business communication. Because the university has no geographic boundaries, its faculty is composed of leading experts from institutions across the United States, including Columbia University, University of California (Berkeley and Santa Barbara), Stanford University, and Purdue University.

"The world of computing and the world of media are converging—the boundaries are melting away. The demand for electronic delivery of college courses should mushroom in the 21st century. Our global society's rate of technological adaptation is both driving that demand and providing the tools to present education via electronic media," states Jones. He believes that the most successful businesses of the future will be those that help solve critical social crises such as the one in education. "The 21st century will not only be a designer century in terms of catering to students' needs, but it will also be a century of expanding reach," Jones continues.[3]

In addition to JIU, other Internet offerings provided by Jones-Knowledge.com include *e*-education, a suite of online learning products and services designed to help colleges, universities, corporations, and other institutions provide high-quality online learning experiences. *E*-education's components include *e*-education online course software, an easy-to-use course development and management product; College Connection, a full-service academic customer service center for faculty, administrators, and students; GetEd.com, a Web site providing listings, enrollment forms, and online payment transactions for institutions offering distance education programs; and *e*-global Library, an online library designed to provide support for online faculty and students.

Jones Knowledge Store, another subsidiary, is in its fourth successful year as a fully deployed e-commerce solution for self-paced learning software and products. "The Knowledge Store focuses exclusively on the growing need for simple training products for those who need to keep up with computer and technology skills. The Knowledge Store offers colleges and universities an e-commerce storefront to operate an online campus bookstore," Jones explains.

MERGING BUSINESS PRINCIPLES WITH STATE GOVERNMENT STRATEGY

State of Ohio

"Our leaders have discovered that unwritten rules count. They continue to place more value on the individual worker and have built a strong relationship with our labor unions—a partnership that is a big breakthrough for us," says Valerie Pike of Ohio's Department of

Administrative Services. "Our Workforce Development Program, an ongoing educational program, allows state workers to expand their skills, and our human resource conferences have increased communications and networking opportunities for state employees across Ohio."

Former Ohio Governor George V. Voinovich, who now represents Ohio in the U.S. Senate, had this to say:

> Ohio was considered a rust belt industrial and economic casualty during the 1970s and 1980s. When I took over as governor in 1991, Ohio had high unemployment and faced more than a billion-dollar budget deficit. My vision was to create a new state business model, restore confidence in the state, and attract significant business and investment opportunities throughout Ohio. We applied the economic philosophy I had used years before as mayor of Cleveland and expanded it to the state level. We called our strategic plan for achieving Ohio's competitive position in the global marketplace Ohio 2000/Ohio First. We realized that we had to develop a top-quality workforce and at the same time set our financial house in order. So we targeted education for tomorrow's leaders and training for today's workforce.

The Governor's Quality Services Through Partnership Program trained nearly 49,000 state employees in quality, with business as a full-time partner at both state and local levels in designing the workforce development programs. At the center of Ohio's One-Stop Employment and Training systems is the statewide skill-based job-matching system, Ohio Job Net, designed by the Ohio Bureau of Employment Services. Companies can place job orders directly over the Internet and find applicants from the more than 300,000 workers listed by name, location, and skills.

Another key element of the turnaround during the administration of Governor Voinovich was the creation of 12 Regional Economic Development Offices within the state. These regional offices serve as outreach centers that provide the delivery of economic development incentives and services to the Ohio business community. "Ohio was recognized as the number one state in the country in new plants and expansions for the 1991–1997 time period. Governor Bob Taft, the Ohio Department of Development, and state leaders are continuing the initiatives we put in place. We truly have a 21st century economy and our workforce development system focuses on continuous improvement and bottom line service. We see a great future for Ohio in the 21st century," Senator Voinovich concludes.

MERGING A BUSINESS MODEL WITH A CHURCH PARADIGM

Willow Creek Community Church

In the early 1970s, a dynamic youth ministry at South Park Church in Park Ridge, Illinois, began using contemporary music, drama, and Bible teaching that high school students could relate to and apply in their everyday life. Their services grew from a handful of teenagers to 1,000 students a night. Inspired by this was one of the ministry leaders, a recent college graduate by the name of Bill Hybels, now the senior pastor at Willow Creek Community Church.

Sensing the need for innovation and creativity in adult services, the youth ministry rented the Willow Creek Movie Theater in Palatine, Illinois, in 1975. The first week's attendance was only 125 people, but persistence paid off. In three years, attendance had grown to 2,000 people. By 1977 it was standing room only in the theater, and 90 acres of farmland were bought in South Barrington, the present location. The campus now covers 155 acres, and the main auditorium of the 352,000-square-foot building seats 4,500 people. Current attendance for the four weekend services (Saturday and Sunday) and the Saturday night Generation X service is between 16,000 and 17,000 people.

Nancy Ortberg, leader of the Generation X ministry at Willow Creek Community Church, speaks about the future of leadership in the church:

> Willow Creek has created a remarkable culture of innovation, leadership, and persistence. It's a unique combination that allows for the development of some of the best and freshest ideas coupled with the hard work and endurance necessary to make them work. The environment here is one of risk taking and reinventing along the way, which requires strong leadership and listening to God.

This generation—Gen X—is growing up in technology. They understand it—it's a part of their lives. The church, however, is not. So if they don't come to church, their technology—Web site, virtual invitations/tours, CD marketing—can be used to bring church to them for their consideration. Whatever future culture shifts offer subsequent generations, how does the church innovate to reach them while at the same time communicating the relevancy of the gospel message? And what does effective leadership in the church look like in the face of so much innovative potential?

Leadership needs to be a nonhierarchical team mode. This allows for the church to utilize a variety of different leadership styles as a team, where maximum ideas and contributions can be made. This sounds easier than it is. It requires humility of spirit *and* cutting-edge thinking. It requires a community of people submitted to the mission *and* highly individualistic pursuits. And all of this works best in an environment of trust—which takes time and is born out of authenticity.

A nonhierarchical model does not mean no one is in charge. Quite the contrary . . . leading a team like this is much like steering a team of bridled but somewhat wild horses. It takes a tremendous amount of energy, strong people insight, and a gentle but firm guiding hand. The result is that the God-given talents, energy, and passion are released in people rather than stifled. It is a delight to be a part of. The leader steers, motivates, releases, steers, *reins in*, questions, and steers. This leadership approach allows the sharpest minds to be part of the mission, vision, and values. It maximizes contribution and ownership, as well as the impact of innovation. In our experience, this model has allowed our team to not only follow the leading of the Holy Spirit but to also let us participate in that fascinating, God-designed paradox in which we are allowed to lead along with Him.

A MILITARY LEADERSHIP MODEL IN THE PUBLIC SCHOOL SYSTEM

Duval County Public Schools

If it were a headline, it might read: "Retired Military Man Takes Public School Plunge!" And plunge he did. Retired Air Force Major General John C. Fryer, Jr. dove right in on his first day as superintendent of Duval County Public Schools (Jacksonville, Florida) by enlisting the assistance of the area's business community. He challenged the business community to build the country's most powerful business alliance in support of public education. The result was phenomenal.

"Within six months, we had a fully functioning Jacksonville Alliance for World Class Education. Fifty of the city's top CEOs are on the Board of Governors and seven of them head the Alliance's various councils. One businessman has already pledged $1 million to help establish a leadership center for professional development, and pledges are coming in now that will raise nearly $2 million for operational programs for the coming year," says Fryer. The Duval County School System has 153 schools, a $1 billion budget, and over 13,000 employees.

The kind of leadership skill demonstrated by this retired Air Force officer has definitely been strengthened by his military career. As Fryer goes on to explain:

> A successful officer progresses through a series of increasingly demanding leadership and staff assignments and is provided with education and training at each stage of development. The officer must be capable of dealing with complex problems of national importance and must often represent the position of his organization to many constituencies, ranging from the local community to Congress and the executive branch.
>
> My last military assignment included leadership of the National War College in Washington. This is the premier joint school in our military professional education system. Its emphasis on national strategy and policy was notably appropriate for a local public official who must continuously walk a tightrope, surrounded by often critical school board members, demanding parents, and large numbers of

students who have insufficient preparation or support for their daily school work.

Innovation and a willingness to change are keys to successful leadership. Fryer has this to add:

> School systems have traditionally been engulfed in issues of process and inputs, with little accountability for output and product. We have established five strategic goals for the district: improve safety and discipline, enhance academic performance, establish accountability at all levels, build learning communities, and develop high performance management systems at the district level and in our 153 schools. The primary academic thrust has been to establish performance standards for all subjects, at all school levels. While completion of this task will take several years, district personnel and the public are beginning to understand the centrality of this requirement for improvement in performance and accountability. Performance standards are embedded in all of our armed services and have long been recognized by the business community as critical to success.

When asked to elaborate on his vision of leadership in the new millennium, Fryer stated:

> The first requirement for leadership is competence. The competence we seek in our schools is in the basic skills needed for success in life. Leaders of school systems in the 21st century must have a clear understanding of the job market and citizenship demands that their students will be facing. Lifelong learning skills and high competency in the fundamentals will be essential for the success of modern students.
>
> Only through the success of public schools will our economy continue to thrive and our children achieve their potential. Today's superintendent must be a true community leader, with the vision, assertiveness, and political and management skills expected of a mayor or a corporate CEO. Large urban school systems are big businesses, expending billions of dollars, and they produce the most important product in our nation.

LEADERSHIP STRATEGIES

✓ Study each of the eight organizational models presented in this chapter.

✓ Identify the model you are now using.

✓ Of the eight models discussed, identify multiple models to blend for meeting organizational goals.

✓ After using blended models for six months, assess any variances in organizational performance.

✓ Determine if these variances can be attributed to model blending.

✓ Decide whether your organization needs to change the mix of models being used or should proceed with the blended paradigm you are now using.

QUESTIONS FOR CONTEMPLATION

1. Does your organization have a pure model that it uses, or has it adopted blended organizational models?

2. If so, which models are being blended?

3. What are the characteristics of each model that is being used?

4. What models would you use in your organization if you could deliberately create a blended paradigm?

5. What initiatives do you need to take to get your ideas implemented?

ENDNOTES

1. For more information about Girl Scouts, call 800-GSUSA4U, or visit their Web site <www.girlscouts.org>.

2. Sam Hill and Glenn Rifkin, *Radical Marketing: From Harvard to Harley, Ten Radical Marketers That Broke the Rules and Made It Big* (New York: Harper Business, 1999).

3. For more information about JonesKnowledge.com, visit its Web site <www.jones knowledge.com>.

STEP 4

Engage the
Whole Person

CHAPTER 10

Incorporating the Whole Person Model

In the past, people were expected to bring only their job skills to the workplace. Now they are asking for help with personal and family problems, and the more progressive organizations are beginning to accommodate them. As I cited in Chapter 8, many enterprises have at least one of the following: children's day care, elder care, or Employee Assistance Programs. Further, career centers in leading-edge organizations help workers maintain their employability. No longer does the organization pay only for skills but it also works to develop and support the whole person.

Figure 10.1 depicts the Whole Person Model (WPM) that I use with organizations to show that the workplace is moving toward androgyny. Those characteristics that once were considered to be typically male or female are combining to produce a non-gender-specific environment.

The WPM indicates that the history of work can be traced back for 10,000 years to nomadic times. For more than 9,900 years, work was mostly physical. In the beginning, work that required physical ability and strength was reserved for males. Men hunted, women gathered. Wars over territory were fought physically; aggression was considered a male characteristic. As time progressed, work continued to be mostly dependent on physical strength. In the 19th century, inventions reduced the need for physical labor; and during the indus-

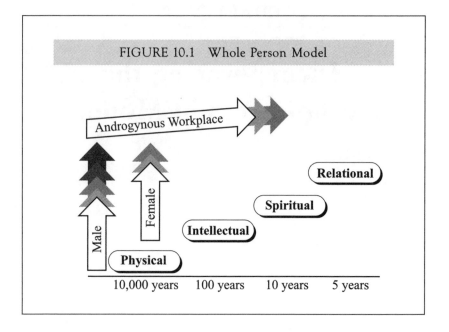

FIGURE 10.1   Whole Person Model

trial revolution, machines replaced much of the physical labor. Knowledge of how to hunt for certain game or how to run machines was necessary for success down through the ages, but not until about 100 years ago did work become highly intellectual. Since the beginning of time, knowledge work has been a small portion of work, but only in 1990 did the world recognize that we truly had entered the knowledge age.

Knowledge work was considered to also be in the male domain in the early years; most accountants and physicians were male, for example. Then women began to enter the ranks of knowledge workers, and it was discovered that, indeed, they could do the work. In the near future, knowledge workers will be equally represented by both men and women. At this point, knowledge work is more complex than physical work ever was, for higher-level thinking processes are involved. However, artificial intelligence (AI) will follow the same path as machines. Just as machines replaced much of the physical labor, AI will eventually replace intellectual work.

Ray Kurzweil, one of our era's greatest inventors, fast forwards his readers in *The Age of Spiritual Machines: When Computers Exceed Human Intelligence* to the year 2029 and states that "a $1,000 unit of computation (in circa-1999 dollars) has the computing capacity of

approximately 1,000 human brains (1,000 times 20 million billion—
that is, 2 times 10^{19} calculations per second."[1]) Will knowledge work
go the way of physical labor? The answer is yes. I believe that work
will be totally redefined. In fact, work will be nothing like we know
it today.

The next question is obvious: How will people make a living?
The answer: creatively. It is difficult to see that far down the road, but
making a living creatively will have political implications. Work as we
know it will disappear. The distribution of wealth may change dramatically. Just as the physically strong were replaced as workplace
heroes by the intellectually gifted, workplace heroes will shift again
during the first quarter of the 21st century to those who are self-governing and relational. To say it another way, the worker elite will be
the introspective and social. As a leader, knowing yourself and relating well to others will be definite and primary requirements for future
success.

For the past ten years, much attention has been dedicated to the
spiritual part of the individual—the inner life. In my seminars, some
of the participants argue that our spiritual selves have always been an
important part of life and that much attention has always been given
to that part of people. I don't disagree that people's spiritual life has
always been important down through the ages. But in postmodern
thought, the past ten years have seen an unprecedented spiritual
search. It is from this realm of human existence that emanate the soft
skills—skills typically considered feminine. But men too must learn
these skills by engaging in a spiritual search.

Overlapping the spiritual realm, as indicated in the WPM, is the
relational aspect of work, once again relegated to the realm of the
female. I personally believe that it is impossible to interrelate unless
one is astute on the intrapersonal (spiritual) level. I cannot conceive
how people can intelligently relate to others until they can first understand themselves. Only in the past five years has the workplace begun
to emphasize the mastery of the spiritual level as a prerequisite to mas-
tering the relational level. In the following paragraphs, I explore how
these levels of maturity exist in the workplace. Great leaders first apply
the principles involved in these levels in their own life and then see
to it that the workers in their organization are progressing on the same
levels of maturity. Until you can function with an integrated mix of
these qualities, it is impossible to have a holistic, androgynous
approach to life and work.

PHYSICAL LEVEL

The workplace continues to reflect shades of the physical part of humanity even though physicality is no longer dominant. Competition for turf, physical violence, and addictions—all can be spiritual problems expressed physically. They reveal that humans express themselves predominately in the physical realm. Just think of the number of addictions that emanate from the most basic of all drives for food, drink, and sex. Eating disorders are at an all-time high. Alcoholism costs organizations billions of dollars per year. And the newest addiction to be cited in the organization is sexual addiction.

With the availability of the Internet (and all the salacious sites available) coupled with high-pressure organizational stress, many people's sexual obsessions are becoming evident—and starting to threaten their careers. According to the National Council on Sexual Addiction and Compulsivity, workplace sexual harassment may be a part of the sexual addict's behavior, which may result in lawsuits, lost productivity, and strained interpersonal relationships. Approximately 83 percent of sexual addicts have such other addictions as alcoholism, eating disorders, or other compulsive behaviors.[2]

The idea of competition signals physical aggression. This concept is becoming more intense in the organizational world; yet it is a holdover from ancient times when there was competition for territory in war. The term *competition* has to do with a form of war; there is a winner and a loser. Physical aggression is being replaced with wars over dominance in the realm of intellectual property. Yet the connotation is similar. Some organizational philosophers are dabbling with the idea of moving from competition to cooperation. Capitalism defies such illusions. As I mentioned in Chapter 3, the DynaForce marketization fosters a purer form of capitalism and thus makes competition even hotter.

The physical realm is alive and well today. However, to remain at that plane without integrating more mature levels would result in totally barbaric organizations.

INTELLECTUAL LEVEL

This is the dominant level in organizations today and is where the action is. Leaders are trying to figure out how to measure knowledge productivity. Conferences are held on methods of motivating knowledge workers. International laws are being written for establishing and protecting rights to intellectual property; the management of intellectual assets is a new frontier. Compensation for knowledge workers far outstrips that of other types of personnel.

Wisdom springs from this level, although it also has a spiritual element. As we defined it earlier, wisdom is a combination of knowledge and vision. Knowledge can be an inner knowing plus intellectual perception. Wisdom now pertains more to the future than to the past. The intellect registers the possibilities and even calculates probabilities. Coupled with internal instinct, the intellect causes great leaders to see the future first. To accomplish this, they must nurture their own intellect and spirit as well as the collective intellect and spirit of the organization.

Business and education are teaming to arrive at a curriculum that prepares students for the work world in which knowledge reigns supreme. Beginning in kindergarten, curriculum must be designed around the discipline of thinking. Innovation usually comes from thinking about a problem in a nontraditional way, an art that will be nurtured in the schools.

Formal education is the preparation ground for knowledge workers. Success is virtually impossible without it. They must *specialize* in something to play a stellar role in the workplace. Then they can find new ways to think about and approach their chosen discipline.

In previous chapters, I addressed the various aspects of knowledge work and knowledge workers. They require more education and complex thinking skills. However, just as physical work has been displaced, so intellectual work will be displaced within 30 years. Great leaders will be planning the organization's move to the next level of maturity to get ahead of the competition.

SPIRITUAL LEVEL

Because this is such a new area of organizational study, I will devote the greater part of this chapter to the spiritual level. The human soul includes the intellectual functions (the mind), feelings (emotions), and intent (will). St. Paul the Apostle in the New Testament of the Holy Bible used a Greek word for *soul* that has the same root as the word *psychology*.[3] The soul in the context I am using it here is the *self*. Comprehension at the level of the soul is at the very least understanding yourself, although it involves much more. The "much more" takes us into intense theological debate and is beyond the scope of this book. If the human is triunal, as many theologians believe, then the soul is one of three parts of the human—the other two parts being the body (physical) and the spirit (eternal). In effect, each human (a spiritual being) exists presently in eternity—a spiritual state. The choice of that spiritual state, or eternity, depends on decisions emanating from the soul (intellect, emotions, and the will).

As a leader, it is important that you know your *self*, and knowing your *self* involves intense introspection. Before we go any further, a series of statements to invoke inner-directed thinking is listed in Figure 10.2. Please complete each one in your own words. They are intentionally open-ended. There is no right or wrong answer. Don't worry about definitions. Let the words mean what you want them to. Take all the time you need to contemplate your answers. It is even better to write them down. Spending time with your *self* is a luxury.

Until you have self-knowledge, it is impossible to be authentic. In my study of the generations, the keyword that was pervasive in my conversations with Generation Yers was *authenticity*. They emphasized a desire to be real and respected leaders who exhibited that quality. Conversely, they lacked respect for leaders who were untruthful or who played roles contrary to their real identity. They were not impressed by people who defined themselves by their job titles or who were arrogant. Perhaps this attitude will become the overriding philosophy in the next decade as Generation Yers continue to have more social and workplace influence.

In 1995, after a journey of self-discovery, Paul Wieand opened the Center for Advanced Emotional Intelligence (AEI) in Ottsville, Pennsylvania, to help leaders to remain true to their real selves and to grow in self-knowledge. Wieand, who holds a Ph.D. in psychology from Temple University in Philadelphia, believes, as does Daniel Goleman, author of best-selling books on emotional intelligence, that understanding your emotions is more important than intellect in becoming a great leader.[4] Emotions are a part of the soul in the context of our study.

Considering the answers you gave to the 17 statements posed in Figure 10.2, let's explore some of the topics.

FIGURE 10.2   Self-Assessment Exercise: Exploring Your Soul

1. My major life purpose on earth is . . .
2. My major strengths are . . .
3. My major weaknesses are . . .
4. I am most fearless when . . .
5. My greatest fears are . . .
6. My favorite workstyle is . . .
7. My best learning style is . . .
8. What I value most is . . .
9. I can make a difference by . . .
10. I feel a sense of peace when . . .
11. If I had unlimited money I would . . .
12. I lose a sense of time when I am . . .
13. I get my discernment of right and wrong from . . .
14. I believe God is . . .
15. My answers to Questions 13 and 14 influence my perspective of ethics by . . .
16. I receive my self-esteem and personal value from . . .
17. My emotions are triggered as follows:

    _____ triggers anger   _____ triggers depression
    _____ triggers sadness   _____ triggers fear
    _____ triggers hate   _____ triggers love
    _____ triggers happiness

Life purpose. If you believe that we all have a definite purpose on earth, then you probably expressed what you think your purpose is. It's good if you can clarify your life purpose in two or three words. Finding your life purpose usually takes quite a bit of trial and error and learning from experience. When you find it, you will know it. It will feel right somehow.

Many baby boomers are looking intently for their purpose as they approach middle age. In their busy lives, they have not had time to explore how they can make a difference and are now setting out to do just that. Many of them are choosing to take early retirement and seek other opportunities in nonprofit and religious institutions. They seek to do social good. The corporate bailout is so profuse that there is a paucity of leaders in succession training in larger corporations.

Workstyles. It amazes me how many people are working in an organization that contradicts their workstyle. Those who would rather work in a casual, laid-back, smaller workplace find they have selected a more formal, large organization. Preferring to work from 6:00 AM to early afternoon, they find themselves locked into an 8:00 AM to 5:00 PM job situation.

What if a worker prefers to work alone and teamwork is the path to greater productivity for the organization? Consider that working in a group may be distracting. In that case, work assignments should take that into consideration, and the leader should make every effort to see that this worker is able to spend some time in individual work.

When a person's desired workstyle fits the actual work environment, that person's productivity increases. Great leaders know this and try as hard as possible to adjust the workplace to reflect individual workstyles.

Learning styles. From the early days of education, it has been assumed that everyone learned in the same way. Higher intelligence existed in those who were verbally and mathematically proficient, experts thought. There was no other measure of learning; college entrance exams, for example, measure mainly verbal and mathematical skills. Those who learned by such other means as visual or musical were considered lower in intelligence.

Dr. Howard Gardner of Harvard University identified seven kinds of intelligence—kinesthetic, verbal, mathematical, musical, spatial, intrapersonal, and interpersonal.[5] Thus, it then seems reasonable that people learn and are intelligent in other ways than verbally and mathematically. The views expressed in the remainder of this section reflect my theories and not those of Dr. Gardner's.

The WPM indicates that people progress on a scale of maturity. As with a dominant intelligence, an individual may be dwelling predominantly on one of the four WPM levels. When the dominant intelligence intersects with the person's present level on the WPM, then the individual can figure out his or her options for learning styles. If a person has a dominant intelligence, yet has not reached the maturity level to realize that intelligence's potential, the individual's learning style may be limited. For example, if an individual has dominant intrapersonal intelligence but has not reached that level on the WPM, then the full potential of intelligence will not be realized. The WPM demands deliberate progression through the stages and an acute awareness of each stage of development. Learning and insight must take place on each level in order to mature to the next level.

If a person's dominant intelligence is mathematical, for instance, and the individual has progressed to relational maturity, the person can learn well either working in groups or by solving problems alone. If the learner had progressed only to the intellectual level, he or she would have a difficult time communicating with others and would probably learn best while studying alone in an isolated environment or applying problems. Interpersonal interaction would be difficult. Had this person not progressed beyond the physical level, he or she would learn better by doing.

The higher the level of maturity one exhibits on the WPM, the more options the individual has for learning styles.

Peace. How did you answer the question about what brings you peace? It is important to know how to create peace in your life to control stress. The chaotic state of today's organizational world causes workers undue stress. Some leaders and workers in the high-tech telecommunications industry report working around the clock on a regular basis under intense deadlines. Continued rightsizings, combined with mergers and acquisitions, have resulted in an all-time high for stress.

Many people try to camouflage stress through the use of alcohol, drugs, or other compulsive behaviors, which only exacerbates the situation. As I discussed earlier, one theory concerning the cause of increased sexual addiction is increased stress. Spiritual problems are, in this case, expressed physically.

If you are self-aware, you will recognize your physical and emotional reaction to stress and take action. One way to reduce stress is to do something that brings you peace. Each of us has a different way to bring peace to our life. I like to take walks in beautiful, quiet gardens or sit by a stream and listen to gently flowing water. In addition, I enjoy hearing a soft wind fluttering through the trees in our backyard. I could sit for hours listening to the birds singing at sunrise. If I am traveling and cannot physically go there, I visualize these places and imagine the sights and sounds.

All these sights and sounds help me sense the eternal and are where I find my personal peace. Your place of peace may be something different. It is important, however, that you find that spot and take time to go there—for your sanity's sake.

Strengths/Weaknesses. I've been consulting in the area of personal development for more than 20 years. During this time, I have been encouraging people to build on their strengths. In this economy, it is imperative to become even better in areas where you are already strong. Our organization urges people to grow based on their strengths.

It is also important to face your weaknesses. After identifying the areas that may cause you to stumble, you then must decide if you should ignore them or spend valuable time and energy improving them. The obvious test for that decision is the question: Is this weakness keeping me from a position of excellence? If so, then do something about it. If not, it may be best to spend your time and energy building on your strengths rather than working on your weaknesses.

I have mentioned success arrogance before. Often, successful people—and also successful organizations—fail to listen. They become so confident in what they think they know that they don't hear feedback concerning their weaknesses. Therefore, they ignore what should be fixed. The prime example is when corporations begin to think they know what is best for the customer and fail to solicit feedback. Arrogance itself is a weakness and normally precedes failure. A wonderful gift you can give yourself is to be honest about your strengths and weaknesses.

Fear. Fear is an emotion that can block excellence. It can even be a barrier to the achievement of your lifelong dreams. Obviously, some fears are real and are to be respected, but most fears are unfounded and it's difficult to find a source. Psychologists label these unfounded types of fears as anxieties. If the late 20th century was the age of anxiety, the 21st century will be called the age of hyperanxiety. It is wise to ask: Are my fears real? How can I overcome them?

You may think that this part of the chapter is not for leaders because leaders are thought not to have fears. All of us, if we are completely honest with ourselves, have fears—sometimes paralyzing fears—at one time or another in our life.

Admittedly, some emotions connected to fear may be clinical in nature—for example, depression. In this case, it is important to see a mental health professional. Various prescription drugs are now available to relieve clinically diagnosed maladies. Most fears can be faced and overcome, and then we are ready to do our best work and make our best contribution to society.

Doing what you like. If you could do anything you wanted in life, what would you do? What a fun question to answer! It allows you to express your hopes and dreams without limitations. Quite often, we lose all track of time while doing something we really enjoy. People who are working in a field they would choose even if money or making a living was not an issue are truly blessed. I personally believe in a designer life—a life that is ideally the one you would live if you had unlimited opportunities. Of course, this kind of life takes planning. It involves aligning what you really want with what is possible. You may wish to retire early, then do what you really want to do. It could be that what you wish to do is inherent in your career. Then you are definitely the lucky one! Some people choose to sacrifice material things to live a freer life. The important thing is to remember that you do have choices. It is also important to remember to balance your choices with your responsibilities.

Remember to prioritize. Several managers, who are also working mothers, have expressed to me that they would really like to stay at home with their children during the day and be with them as they grow up. None of these women are single mothers. They have told me that although the budget would be tight, family income would be adequate if they no longer worked outside the home. They feel they must decide between material wants or needs and motherly desires. Participating in a flexible workplace may be able to help in this case. Perhaps these working mothers could job share or telecommute. I suggest that they propose such arrangements to their organization—even if they are not openly offered. Often, these conditions can be arranged even when the woman is in a managerial position. The important point is that, in the future, women leaders will be more flexible in the workplace and free to choose to participate in both career and family.

Ethics/Character. You probably thought carefully when considering where you get your sense of right and wrong from. Your definitions of *right* and *wrong* are also related to what you think about a

Higher Power, your God. Think of this in the broader context. As organizations become predominantly multicultural—and as the relational aspect of maturity becomes more important—it is imperative to have common agreement about the definition of *ethics*.

In a study sponsored by the American Society of Chartered Life Underwriters and Chartered Financial Consultants and the Ethics Officers Association, it was discovered that a distinct majority (60 percent) of respondents believed that ethical dilemmas are avoidable in business. This is a very hopeful trend. In the 1970s and 1980s, it was popularly believed that business and ethics could not reasonably coexist. Today, however, it is believed that ethical dilemmas can be reduced.[6]

Ethical decisions are often sources of internal conflict. The situation may be personal; for example, when you know that your best friend's husband is having an affair, and you are close to both of them, should you tell her? You are a team leader and know that a member of your work team is generating incorrect data in a report to higher-level company leadership. How should you handle this situation? Your project is under intense deadline. You are tempted to relax quality standards in a couple of places. You feel that the results will be harmless. What would you do?

Most character-building situations aren't easy to resolve. They require deep soul searching and the courage to do what you think to be right. Some decisions are tough. For example, your oldest daughter is graduating from high school at the same time that you need to be in Europe to consummate the biggest contract in company history. That causes terrible internal conflict, especially if neither event can be moved to another time. Your choice—plus your ability to define and explain your reasoning to the person most affected by the event you do not choose—really defines your character. It boils down to balancing what you value more coupled with the greater long-term impact of missing one of the events. Tough decision!

Values. To align your values with reality as a leader, you must have a sense of what is deeply important to you. It also helps to know your core competencies. To determine if you are on target in synchronizing your values with your work environment, take a moment to fill in the exercise in Figure 10.3. Great leaders are able to synchronize their values with their work and want their workers to do the same. Both leaders and workers will find this exercise useful.

FIGURE 10.3   Self-Assessment Exercise: Assessing Your
Preferences and Core Competencies

1. I prefer working with (in rank order) ___people ___machines ___data.
2. I prefer working ___independently ___on a team.
3. I prefer a work environment that is ___static ___changing.
4. My three greatest work values are (in rank order) ___freedom ___interdependence ___power ___money ___self-actualization (meaningful, purposeful work) ___self-esteem (positive self-value) ___security.
5. I prefer work that is (in rank order) ___cognitive ___manual ___relational.
6. The seven things I enjoy doing most in my work are:
   ___calculate ___analyze ___synthesize ___correlate (data) ___teach ___learn ___lead (influence) ___follow ___manage (plan, organize, direct, control) ___assemble (things) ___create ___implement ___solve (problems) ___relate (to people) ___write ___confront ___research ___decide ___negotiate ___initiate ___present (ideas to an audience) ___talk ___listen ___compete ___envision ___explore (the unknown) ___other _____.
7. My five greatest competencies are to ___calculate ___analyze ___synthesize ___correlate (data) ___teach ___learn ___lead (influence) ___follow ___manage (plan, organize, direct, control) ___assemble (things) ___create ___implement ___solve (problems) ___relate (to people) ___write ___confront ___research ___decide ___negotiate ___initiate ___present (ideas to an audience) ___talk ___listen ___compete ___envision ___explore (the unknown) ___other _____.
8. Does my work involve my preferences and core competencies expressed in statements 1 through 7?
9. In order to align my preferences and core competencies with my work, I should

_____

_____

In completing the last statement in Figure 10.3, you will have to make some difficult decisions if your preferences and core competencies are not in alignment with your present work environment. After considering priorities and responsibilities, it is important to your future well-being that you have the courage to take action!

Faith-Friendly Organizations

Remember that I defined the soul earlier and said that it has eternal significance. By *eternal,* I mean that timeless and spaceless dimension beyond this physical life. How you connect eternally depends on your concept of God (or no God). In this domain, your beliefs are based on faith. Spirituality is a unique and private arena for each person. To some people, spirituality means nurturing the soul. To others, it may mean cultivating their ecclesiastical faith. According to George Gallop, Jr. of the Princeton Research Center, 82 percent of Americans say that they feel the need to experience spiritual growth.[7]

Faith-friendly workplaces are the newest link to workplace wholeness. Workers are no longer content with leaving their faith at home and bringing the remainder of their self to the workplace. They want to be present in both body and spirit. People want their life to have value. Much spirituality in the workplace involves synchronizing the worker's values with the organization's mission. Such values as social consciousness, trust, integrity, unity, justice, mercy, and life balance cut across all of the major religious belief systems.

Workers are increasingly open about their religious beliefs in the organization. They want to be able to practice what they believe at work. Title VII of the Civil Rights Act of 1964 requires employers of 15 or more people to *reasonably accommodate* an employee's religious observance or practice unless there would be *undue hardship* on the employer's business. The desire for spiritual openness coupled with at least half the workforce not attending any organized religious services makes the workplace a major conduit for spiritual training on the employee's own time. Classes in Islam as well as studies of the Koran, the Bible, and the Torah are taking place before the workday begins or on lunch breaks in organizations across America. Some organizations are building special spaces for meditation, prayer, or quiet time. Chaplains, who have long been employed by the military and hospitals, now have offices in business organizations to help workers with their spiritual needs.

Marketplace Ministries. "Almost 19 years ago, I began sensing a great need in the workplace for workers to feel they are valued—that someone cares about them and their problems. I had been an army chaplain, and, as a retired colonel, I wanted to take the military ministry concept into the secular workplace—to be with people where they are," says Gil A. Stricklin, founder and president of Marketplace Ministries (MMI) in Dallas, Texas. Stricklin expands on the theme:

> Since people spend the greatest amount of their time at work, I wanted to help them build their sense of satisfaction in their jobs and in their lives. Statistics today show that more than 50 percent of the workforce does not belong to any religious organization, less than 37 percent of Americans go to church once a week, and only 21 percent attend a church where they belong. So there is a great need to raise an umbrella of compassion over people and management on the job—that is the mission of Marketplace Ministries.

Marketplace Ministries offers corporations a proactive Employee Assistance Program (EAP). "It is a lot like a health plan or a spiritual 911 service. Our chaplains have pagers and cell phones and are accessible 24 hours a day to employees of our client companies. Each chaplain averages one call every 4 hours with over 800,000 total contracted service hours since 1984," explains Stricklin. An independent nonprofit organization, MMI staffs chaplains at 400 sites in 200 different companies. Its ministry has expanded from serving 500 employees and family members in 1984 to more than 170,000 in 180 cities spread across 30 states today.

Stricklin explains further:

> Our chaplains are MMI employees, and we are currently adding three to five chaplains per week. The chaplains work 20 to 30 hours each week, and 40 full-time coordinators serve as divisional and regional directors. We are nondenominational, and our number of minority chaplains is growing. The chaplain's ministry team needs to fit the mix of company employees. Our top line is people's needs, and our bottom line is to meet those individual needs.
>
> One of the most visible changes America is experiencing in the 21st century is the increase of violence in the

workplace. Our client companies believe the chaplaincy program is good business and helps attract workers in a time of stiff competition and low unemployment. We also believe it is an anecdote for workplace homicide. If disgruntled workers have someone to turn to, hate and conflict can be defused by love, prayer, and a helping hand.

DalMac. DalMac is a Texas-based firm providing construction, real estate, and property management services. Since its founding in 1958, the firm's value-focused and collaborative approach has successfully delivered services to clients in the office, institutional, retail, industrial, manufacturing, hospitality, and multifamily markets. As part of the firm's commitment to fostering a supportive team environment both internally and externally, DalMac employs Marketplace Ministries to offer spiritual and emotional support to the firm's 295 associates. The DalMac leadership team elected to make these chaplain services available in an effort to better respond to employees' needs in a personal and confidential manner. According to Kurt Petersen, vice president of DalMac Construction Company's Dallas division, "Having chaplains as part of our team enables DalMac's leadership to offer support from trained professionals who are focused and committed to helping employees in need or in a crisis situation."

Hatfield. Joy Ziegler is a chaplain at Hatfield Incorporated in Hatfield, Pennsylvania, and is also an area coordinator for Marketplace Ministries Inc. "We have 12 chaplains here at Hatfield, and everything we do is at the employees' request. We are currently conducting a Bible study for executives, comparing leadership concepts in a business book with a study of the Book of Nehemiah from the Old Testament," states Ziegler. "When I began this job, I had to cultivate my listening abilities because people's greatest need is for someone to listen to them. In fact, one day an employee came in and talked for more than 30 minutes while I just actively listened. He then thanked me over and over for what I had done to help him," Ziegler laughingly explains. "The employees see us on the job every day, and they get to know us and trust us."

Many workers want to discuss marriage problems, and they know the chaplain keeps this confidential. The chaplains also help employees through their most difficult times:

One employee and his wife had separated, but decided to get back together as they continued facing and working out their problems with the chaplain. Also, when there are medical emergencies, we go right to the emergency room to be with employees or members of their family. For example, the five-year-old daughter of an employee needed heart surgery, and the couple's family all lived in New York. We visited with them every day and became their support group until she was able to go home months later.

Last year the sister of one of our employees, a young man in his early 30s, was in a terrible accident. Several of our chaplains were there at the hospital for him when she went into a coma. Then when the doctors said there was no hope for her, the chaplain stayed with the young man while he made the decision to disconnect life-support equipment and was with him when she passed away. We also go to the plant floor when an employee dies to tell coworkers and be there for counseling with them. Hatfield understands that the employees know that management really cares.

Interstate Batteries. Workplace chaplaincy outreach is multifaceted. "Many employees see more of their fellow workers than they see of their own families. So it is important to foster a caring, familylike environment at work," says Henry Rogers, chaplain at Interstate Batteries in Dallas. Examples of employee empathy are many. "Recently, a worker's father was killed, and she had no money to fly home for the funeral. Another employee came to me and handed me an envelope with money for airline tickets," Rogers continues. "Don't use my name," the employee said, "but make sure she is able to go to the funeral."

Rogers tells of another occasion when a tragic accident took the life of an employee's three-year-old child. There was such an outpouring of love from employees, not only around the time of the funeral, but also later in helping with fence repairs, gardening, and other activities to prepare the employee's house for sale. Interstate Batteries has had a full-time chaplain since 1988, and it has expanded worker involvement to active community service in the chaplaincy area. Once a quarter, employees conduct a service at the Jesse Dawson State Jail, and they often help serve evening meals at the Union Gospel Mission. "It gives our people such a good feeling to see many of the homeless come through the food line wearing clothing our people had provided through clothing drives. This is really part of our extended family caring."

Industrial chaplaincy groups. Dr. Diana C. Dale, executive director of the National Institute of Business and Industrial Chaplains (NIBIC), says that contemporary industrial chaplaincy is often cited as having been pioneered by R. G. LeTourneau, who established full-time industrial chaplaincy at his plants in Illinois, Georgia, and Mississippi in 1941. "Other business owners soon followed suit," states Dr. Dale. "The NIBIC was incorporated in 1976 as the professional organization for business and industrial chaplains. In 1985, the United AutoWorkers (UAW) initiated a program to provide industrial chaplaincy to its union members. The UAW program is organized by region and continues to grow with more than 300 chaplains active in plants across North America.

The Institute of Worklife Ministry, the workplace chaplaincy training division of the Worklife Institute based in Houston, Texas, was founded by Dr. Dale in 1988. "Also, international communications among industrial chaplaincy professionals is building with ongoing networking linkages among national organizations' leadership. At this time, there are more than 4,000 persons in North America actively engaged in worklife-directed ministry, and this diverse field of service is rapidly expanding," Dr. Dale concludes.

The Increasing Diversity of Religious Practice

Each week you will find Bible study classes, prayer breakfasts, spiritual discussion groups, and joint Christian-Jewish meetings on Capitol Hill.[8] Congress holds these types of gatherings during the early morning, at break times, during lunch, or in the evenings.

Sensitivity to all beliefs is the newest component of diversity training. An increasing number of cases of religious harassment are being reported. As people become more spiritual and varied in their faith, they will demand the freedom to carry out their religious practices in the workplace. For example, Muslim women wish to wear headscarves at work, and Muslims in the workplace wish to pray at the mosque on Fridays. Some Christians do not want to work on Sundays. Some Jews oppose working on their Sabbath. Workers are wearing jewelry depicting various religious symbols such as the Christian cross. Employees even want to talk about their religion during work hours. Title VII of the Civil Rights Act of 1964, as defined earlier, allows religious activities so long as no undue hardship is placed on employers. If there is not undue hardship on the employer and the employer refuses to accommodate employees' religious practices, then religious discrimination complaints can be filed with the Equal Employment Opportunity Commission (EEOC).

From 1991 to 1998 there was a 50 percent increase in religious discrimination charges filed with the EEOC.[9] Although small compared with filings for sexual discrimination, religious harassment could very well be the next big area of litigation for organizations. Over 80 percent of people in America are much like me in claiming to be followers of Jesus Christ—Christians. For several generations, Christians and Jews dominated the American workplace. The spiritual culture was relatively homogeneous. Therefore, holidays were geared to the Judeo-Christian heritage. However, a growing population of Muslims, Buddhists, and Hindus is coming into the workplace. With so much diversity, employers must gear up for a wealth of varied faiths whose followers are eager to integrate their beliefs into their place of employment.

RELATIONAL LEVEL

Once individuals understand themselves, they are better equipped to understand others in progressing relationships. Where two or more people have had to work together, relational needs exist. Until recently, however, no one realized that self-understanding is a prerequisite for effective interpersonal exchange.

During the last decade much emphasis has been placed on self-directed work teams. Several leaders have reported to me that their teams are not working well because people lack the skills to be self-governing while interacting with a team. My answer to this problem is to back up and start at the spiritual level. Train the people to understand themselves on a deep plane and help them to acquire self-governance skills. Then the team can function more smoothly. I firmly believe that in 90 percent of the cases, team members don't have the spiritual insight necessary for teamwork. They are ill prepared for what is expected of them. Because the spiritual level has been largely neglected in the workplace, workers are not ready for the relational level.

Volumes have been written on communications and how to deal with certain personality types. The objective of this section is not to rehash that literature. My major goal here is to ask you to analyze the interaction between yourself and another person while thinking, *If I say what is on my mind, how will the other party perceive the statement?* In addition, individuals familiar with their own emotional triggers should be aware that certain statements or questions have a specific effect on others and can learn to control their responses.

Good relationships are built on mutual respect, which requires civility to one another. Companies realize that employee behavior is important to the organization's image and directly affects the bottom line. They are going to great lengths to teach manners and international etiquette to all workers—including executives. Success depends on it. Even business schools are offering courses to polish the relational skills of their students, whose future careers will be enhanced by the good image they portray.[10]

Courtesy and sensitivity to others must be genuine to last. When people try to fake these qualities, they end up in a paradox—acting in a way that is incongruent with their true feelings. Such cases result in eventual relational breakdown.

Heather (not her real name) is a group design leader at a software development company. Her social abilities are outstanding, and she usually finds it easy to connect with others. However, she is very concerned with being liked by almost everyone and has a reputation for going out of her way to subdue interpersonal conflict. The leader of her department, Elgina (not her real name), is arrogant, disrespectful to most people, thinks she has all the answers, and wants things on her terms. When she needs help, she demands it rather than asking for it politely. For example, even though Heather is holding a group meeting, Elgina walks into the room proclaiming, "I need you in my office right now." Elgina acts as if Heather's meeting is not nearly as important as the meeting Elgina is calling Heather into. Of course, Heather begins to suffer internal conflict. Should she dismiss her own meeting and reconvene at another time or politely tell Elgina that she will be at her meeting when she wraps up this one? This is a tough call. Heather will knowingly anger Elgina and possibly face retaliation if she does the latter. However, if she gives in without first trying to draw a boundary, she becomes an enabler to Elgina's inappropriate behavior. What would you do in this case?

Heather surprises us. Because she knows that she has trouble setting boundaries, she has been seeing a counselor for help in that area. The supportive counselor is encouraging Heather to take risks. With that in mind, Heather politely replies to Elgina, "Thank you for alerting me about your meeting. I will be finished with my meeting in less than a half hour, and then I will be able to join you."

To make that kind of reply, Heather must have high self-esteem and be able to confront the possible anger and retaliation that Elgina will dispense. She must be confident enough to know that she can transfer to another position or find work outside the company should Elgina decide to make things miserable for her. Heather has the strength to take that risk. In this case, Heather's success will come from her good relational skills, her ability to take what was once a weakness and work through it, and self-esteem that helps her realize that her career is inside herself, not with any one organization. With this in mind, she is free from unnecessary control from others.

Relational courtesy presupposes that people operate with a common set of values. Therefore, genuine courtesy is as much spiritual as it is relational. The aforementioned common values—truth, honesty, justice, mercy, and mutual respect—must be held in common across cultures for courtesy to exist.

As the world continues to democratize and organizations follow suit through greater worker empowerment, courtesy will be the key to balancing freedom and restraint. In a free society, courtesy is the only thing that builds an invisible wall between one person's rights and another's freedoms. Great leaders recognize this and promote it in their organizations.

LEADERSHIP STRATEGIES

✓ Make a conscious decision to get in touch with your inner life.

✓ Take time to visit with yourself by spending ample time completing the 17 statements in the Spiritual Level section of this chapter.

✓ Reflect on ways that you can become more spiritually balanced.

✓ Initiate a program in your organization that provides help for workers to explore their inner self.

✓ Provide organizational chaplains and Employee Assistance Programs for spiritual support.

✓ Implement guidelines for organizational ethics and enforce them.

QUESTIONS FOR CONTEMPLATION

1. On which level is work concentrated in your organization—physical, intellectual, spiritual, or relational?

2. Is your organization progressing toward an androgynous workplace?

3. Does your organization emphasize spiritual awareness? In what ways?

4. How are you using spiritual maturity to help yourself relationally?

5. Would it be helpful to introduce a chaplaincy program into your organization?

6. Are Employee Assistance Programs available in your organization?

7. What three specific actions could your organization take to implement the Whole Person Model?

8. Does your organization promote high levels of ethical behavior?

9. What ethics policies need to be addressed to improve the compliance rate in your organization?

ENDNOTES

1. Ray Kurzweil, *The Age of Spiritual Machines: When Computers Exceed Human Intelligence* (New York: Viking Press, 1999), 220.

2. National Council on Sexual Addiction and Compulsivity, "Consequences of Sexual Addiction and Compulsivity," 8 September 1999, Web page <www.ncsac.org/article4.htm>.

3. Frank Minirth, M.D., Paul Meier, M.D., and Stephen Arterburn, M.Ed., *The Complete Life Encyclopedia* (Nashville: Thomas Nelson Publishers, 1995), 551.

4. Pamela Kruger, "A Leader's Journey," *Fast Company*, June 1999, 118.

5. Howard Gardner, *Frames of Mind* (reprint, New York: Basic Books, 1993).

6. *Sources and Consequences of Workplace Pressure: Increasing the Risk of Unethical and Illegal Business Practices.* A study sponsored by the American Society of Chartered Life Underwriters and Chartered Financial Consultants and the Ethics Officers Association, 1997.

7. George Gallop, Jr., "The Growing 'Faith Factor'," *The Dallas Morning News*, 26 December 1998, 1G. Reprinted with permission of *The Dallas Morning News*.

8. Catalina Camina, "Spirituality on the Hill," Washington Bureau of *The Dallas Morning News*, 17 February 1996, 1G. Reprinted with permission of *The Dallas Morning News*.

9. Statistics for 1991, *The Futurist*, March 1999. Used with permission of the World Future Society, 7910 Woodmont Avenue, Bethesda, Maryland 20814. The 1998 statistics were obtained from Chicago Associated Press newswire "Religion in the Workplace: A Growing Legal Issue," *McKinney Courier-Gazette*, McKinney, Texas, 21 May 1999, 5.

10. Kathryn F. Clark, "Diamonds in the Rough," *Human Resource Executive* (18 June 1999): 38–43.

STEP 5

Ignite Innovation

CHAPTER 11

Trumping the Competition

Innovation is the key to continued prosperity. Although the United States is experiencing a lengthy economic boom, its capacity for innovation per capita is losing ground. Ranking first in 1995 in innovation among 17 countries, the United States is projected to drop to fifth place by 2005 if present trends continue, according to the Organization for Economic Cooperation and Development (OECD).[1] To compete effectively in international markets, nations as well as organizations must make innovation a priority.

In Figure 4.1, I introduced the Organizational Chaos Model showing that a system or an organization (which is itself a system) can be thrown into chaos when the rules, structure, and/or speed of the system's components are changed. The same principles can be used to overcome the organization's competition. The goal is for your organization to change the rules, structure, and speed of its industry so that your competitors are thrown into chaos. Because your organization initiated the change, it more than likely understands the new rules and structure introduced into the marketplace as it copes with changes in speed. Temporarily at least, your organization will be ahead of the competition. This technique has been used by the military since ancient times. The idea is to confuse the enemy. While the opponent is digging out of the confusion, the organization in the offensive position seizes the dominant position.

One contemporary technique that changes the marketplace rules, structure, and speed is innovation—an organization's trump card. When the microchip was invented, Intel was able to gain power over the competition because it capitalized on an innovation. Microsoft innovated the concept of a dominant operating system in personal computers. Delta was one of the first airlines to fly the jet plane—a tremendous invention in the airline industry. By capitalizing on innovations, these companies were able to become leaders in their industries while their competitors were temporarily in chaos trying to find their way out. In today's marketplace, innovation is a survival tool. If an organization is offering the same products and services in the same way that it did three years ago, it's on its way to obsolescence or may already be obsolete. Let's answer three questions about innovation.

What is innovation? My personal definition is derived from working with hundreds of organizations and extensive research on the subject. *Innovation* is the tangible result of creativity—the process that produces one or more innovations. Creativity is difficult to measure, but innovation is a product or service that is easily defined and measured.

Why is innovation necessary? It is needed for survival and sustainability. Competition is so stiff in the global marketplace that organizations not nurturing innovation will soon find themselves unable to respond to changing customer demands. Conversely, those organizations that make innovation a priority can dominate their industry and experience positive growth. Organizations in the 21st century must foster innovation.

How can an organization achieve a high degree of innovation? Innovation does not happen by itself. It must be intentionally cultivated. Great leaders realize this and work to develop an organization friendly to innovative endeavors. This effort involves allocating a budget adequate for innovative activities, establishing a physical environment that promotes creativity, eliminating creativity inhibitors, recruiting creative people, grasping the big picture, involving the whole person, promoting new thinking, training experientially, and nurturing autonomy. Let's take a closer look at these nine factors.

THE NINE FACTORS OF INNOVATION

1. Adequate Budget

Research and development (R&D) requires an investment of time and money. Some organizations, for example, allocate as much as 15 to 20 percent of their annual budget to R&D.

Innovation always occurs with the end user in mind. Organizations constantly examine their products, services, and distribution systems in looking for ways to make them more user friendly. Improved value to the customer is foremost in the minds of great leaders, as is faster distribution. This may mean making changes to present products and services or introducing new ones.

E-commerce. The most sweeping innovation in decades is e-commerce, the conducting of commerce via the Internet—a revolutionary process. Organizations that are not prepared to take advantage of e-commerce will be left behind in the marketplace. According to business communications strategist Ginger L. Ebinger of the In Group in Allen, Texas:

> E-commerce is here to stay. Industry watchers predict, however, that many of the e-tailers doing business today will be gone tomorrow. Why? Because they are not reliable. And when an e-tailer is not reliable, the customers won't come back. It's that simple. And that's hard. Take a lesson from the pros. Pure-play Internet stores are performing better than traditional retailers who go online. They've learned how to build compelling Web sites and strategies that generate demand. They know how to get browsers in the front door and turn those browsers into buyers. And, they know that to get repeat buyers, you must aim for satisfied customers.
>
> To keep satisfied customers, you must provide outstanding customer service—every time, all the time. To get the products and services from the people who provide them to the people who buy them requires that you have an order-processing system that works. The back-end infrastructure that handles every detail—from filling an order to

authorizing credit cards to handling returns—is critical to an e-tailer's success. The entire experience—from buying a product online to having it delivered at the front door—must be positive for the customer. Only then will an e-tailer achieve the success necessary to remain competitive in the growing world of e-commerce.

Educational institutions. It is often difficult for educational institutions to move beyond the learning processes they have practiced for many years, but some are daring to make the change.

I discovered a unique environment in a thriving city just north of Dallas—McKinney, Texas. In the early 1990s a group of McKinney Independent School District (MISD) educators under the leadership of Dr. Jack Cockrill, the district superintendent, applied for and received a one-of-a-kind $5.5 million grant from the U.S. Department of Education to create a school of the future. They named the school the Academic Competitiveness through Technology (ACT) Academy. The concept was so successful that taxpayers now support the school as a viable part of the MISD.

I have had the opportunity to tour this facility. It has the capacity for 300 learners from ages 5 to 18, which is a representative sample of the entire MISD student population. An indication of the success of this academy is that 100 percent of the learners go on to enroll in an institution of higher education. The learning, which makes extensive use of technology, is self-paced and guided by facilitators. Many students complete the high school program in three years. Some learners are even attending college simultaneously with completing the high school curriculum. Not only are the learners given the courses that are offered on-site at ACT Academy, but the virtual high school also offered through ACT Academy allows them to choose among 40 credit courses from all over the world. Susan Germann, ACT Academy's director, stated: "The goal of ACT Academy is to create independent lifelong learners through ever-increasing use of and expertise with technology. We are very aware of business principles here at ACT. We realize that the student is our customer, and everything we do has that customer uppermost in mind."

No grades are given as they are in the traditional school setting. Instead, learners maintain a portfolio that is reviewed four times a year. "There is heavy involvement of parents in the learner's education. The team approach to learning is important at the ACT Academy. Students are allowed to initiate many of their own learning activities," Germann told me. I noticed that a great deal of freedom was allowed, but the walkways were quiet, and there seemed to be no discipline problems. Even small children are taught self-governing strategies and are expected to act responsibly.

A mature young woman, Megan Taylor, the elected student representative for Sherwood Forest (the section representing traditional grades four and five) guided me on an hour-and-a-half tour of the academy. I was impressed with her knowledge and very confident, kind demeanor. "What I like best about this academy is the creativity we are allowed to have," she told me. "It's not like every other traditional school. In fact, lots of people think it's a private school, but it's not. Learners have a lot of control. We have direct access to the Academy's director if we first get permission from the facilitator and the director's door is open. I like that."

This example of the ACT Academy project demonstrates what a few forward-thinking educators can produce—even in a relatively small city. Although McKinney is experiencing unprecedented growth at this time, when the idea for the ACT Academy was conceived, McKinney's population was only about 25,000. The school is so successful that a group from Walt Disney came to visit the academy to gather information before constructing their futuristic school in Celebration, their residential community just outside Orlando, Florida.

Pharmaceutical companies. In the present competitive race, commercial companies are constantly introducing new products and services. Pharmaceutical companies spend billions of dollars a year on R&D and are continually bringing out new disease preventatives and controls. "Their success in development is largely the result of managing risks in the quest to launch quality of life–enhancing pharmaceuticals," states Bonnie Kirschenbaum, M.S., FASHP, a health care consultant in Santa Monica, California.

According to Kirschenbaum:

> Desirable therapeutic outcomes the industry is striving to achieve include curing the patient's disease, elimination or reduction of the patient's symptoms, preventing or slowing the progression of the disease, prevention of the disease or of a symptom, diagnosis of a disease, and avoidance of drug-related problems.

Clearly, early appropriate drug intervention can reduce the need for more expensive and potentially complicated medical or surgical treatments. Many proactive
thinkers have looked not only at the major trends in pharmaceutical development but also in the way that pharmacy
itself will be practiced. Automation and information technology will replace the majority of the task-oriented dis-
pensing activities, leaving the pharmacist free to provide
and coordinate the continuity of care, to utilize these mag-
nificent health care resources effectively, and to ensure continuous patient follow-up. The impact of pharmaceutical
care on a patient's physical, social, and emotional well-
being is of utmost importance.

Software companies. Software companies are continually up-
grading their packages as well as introducing new ones. It's hard to
keep up with the many innovations in the telecommunications and
electronics industries. The caveat seems to be innovate or be left behind. Because products and services have an ever-shortening shelf
life, money must be invested to stay innovative.

Creativity. Employers of the 1,000 largest U.S. companies are
more actively promoting creativity among workers, according to a
recent poll developed by Robert Half International (RHI). Of the 150
executives surveyed, 89 percent said their companies are doing more
now than they did five years ago to encourage employee creativity and
innovation.

How important is innovation in today's marketplace? "Extremely
so," states Lynn Taylor, vice president and director of research of RHI.
"Creativity is the difference between an organization's surviving and
thriving in a fast-paced competitive environment. Leaders constantly
must look ahead and build a better mousetrap. They must be unen-
cumbered by historical policies, procedures, and approaches."

RHI, the world's largest staffing service specializing in the
accounting, finance, and information technology fields, has more than
240 offices in North America, Europe, and Australia. Taylor collabo-
rated with CEO Max Messmer on *Human Resource Kit for Dummies*
(IDG Books Worldwide, 1999), which addresses the new paradigm for
hiring. "As hiring managers interview job candidates, they should ask
applicants to provide examples of how they infused creativity into a

project. They should also ask candidates' references about their creative ideas and performance," continues Taylor.

"The Internet and e-commerce are having an impact on every organization racing to market in a digital world. So we need not only long-term innovation but creativity every day in how we approach our jobs. The organization must foster a creative environment and hire employees who are positive, enthusiastic, and energetic in their outlook," Taylor concludes.

2. Physical Environment

Open, pleasant, and inclusive are all adjectives descriptive of an environment that promotes creativity. As I mentioned earlier, creativity is the process that produces innovation. For creativity to flourish, the atmosphere must be conducive.

One factor to remember is that creativity is natural in all of us. Some people have used this talent more than others and have therefore developed their creativity to a more mature level. Consider children. What do they need to be creative? Not much. Maybe a natural setting, a few props, ample play time, and a vivid imagination. Adults are not much different. Taking a journey into the mind of a child is helpful in learning to create an environment fit for an inventive adult.

Light fosters energy and optimism. It provides natural stimulation for ideas. For the four decades preceding the 1990s, buildings were designed without many windows in order to improve air-conditioning efficiency. Windows were thought to create possible distractions in schools. Because of the cost savings and increasing quality of artificial lighting, structures became self-contained units that blocked nature from view. Today, architects understand the need for natural lighting, so buildings again have windows that offer a view of the outside world.

Smart organizations are creating courtyards and gardens for the workers to enjoy. Greenbelts and colorful plants stimulate creativity. In addition, natural plants interact with the environment to provide a healthier atmosphere—unless one is allergic to a particular plant. Allergies need to be taken into consideration when designing an invigorating milieu.

More and more contemporary buildings are not only offering workers a beautiful outside view but also office interiors that provide wonderful views of atriums, fountains, and greenery. Although totally enclosed and air-conditioned, these environments offer a sense of openness and flow.

Workers should be motivated to personalize their work areas. Whatever they feel reduces their stress and increases their creative energies should be allowed in their space as long as it is not offensive and does not detract from the organization's cultural message. Favorite paintings, pictures of the family, inspirational works—all have special meaning to certain people and motivate them to be creative.

What about designing a creative room? The space could hold as many as 50 people and have the capability of housing every piece of technology the organization could imagine and afford—equipment for computer games, audio/visual technology, videoconferencing, access to the Internet, and anything else that might be stimulating. Creative teams would be encouraged to bring in children's toys when holding their creative sessions there. For example, if a cosmetics company is trying to design new colors for nail polish and lipstick, employees might bring in flowers and vegetables, paint samples, and crayons—and anything else that might provide color ideas—as well as suggestions for naming the new colors. In designing a new marketing program, the participants might bring movie videos, comic books, reference materials, and even some old-fashioned board games while letting ideas incubate. Seemingly unrelated children's toys and props can promote novel, useful ideas.

Color is also important. Yellow, for example, promotes optimism. It represents sunlight and brightness. Red might encourage boldness while blue nourishes serenity. Physical activity areas are also helpful. Volleyball and basketball courts, putting greens, and treadmills are popping up in and around office buildings. When stress levels become high or after-meal sluggishness sets in, using physical activity areas helps people to reenergize.

Finally, some office areas look more like family rooms than workspaces. Overstuffed couches, lounge chairs, video games, and tables for board games are placed for workers to conveniently take a break from their tasks. By structuring this casual atmosphere as well as promoting more casual, tasteful dress, organizations are designing the workplace to foster what creativity is all about—innovation.

You might say, "I am a leader—a great one at that—but I cannot construct a new building and invest hundreds of thousands of dollars in landscaping beautiful gardens just for the sake of creativity." Well, you don't have to. Get creative! As you read this section, what can you implement that fits realistically into your budget? A splash of paint, a room dedicated to creativity, a casual furniture area—all can be inexpensive and effective. These ideas can work anywhere. Your imagination is your only limitation.

3. The Elimination of Creativity Inhibitors

Several years ago I was called into a Fortune 100 company to assess its readiness for the 21st century. This company, very successful for 50 years, had forgotten how to foster creativity. When I began to tour the facilities where the supposedly creative people worked, I sensed the subdued atmosphere. The building was dimly lit and decorated in muted colors. There was total quiet. Every wall in every office looked alike. All the people dressed much the same.

When I began to talk with them individually, it was easy to determine that the employees were not very optimistic about the company's future. Many of them expressed to me that they felt stifled by company rules about everything from the dress code to the way they were not allowed any individuality in their office space. Pessimism prevailed. I came home from that assignment aghast that such a powerful company could have allowed itself to get into that situation. The company, in my opinion, had a declining future.

This story, however, has a happy ending. The company's leaders later became open to suggestions and began to change. Why? Not necessarily because I informed them that they were not 21st-century ready, but because within just a few months their market share began to suffer. There's nothing like a loss in market share to grab a leader's attention. Backed into a corner, the company then began to make necessary changes to regain its vibrancy and again compete in its dog-eat-dog marketplace.

This company illustrates an organization filled with creativity inhibitors. For the sake of innovation, these roadblocks had to be removed. Some of the factors I noticed that were impeding creativity were the employees' mistrust of management, the bleak office atmosphere, a strict dress code at all times, and the lack of imagination in office decoration.

The employees told me their leaders were arrogant and their methods reflected the command-and-control governance model, which I believe caused mistrust of the higher ranks. The employees were afraid to be creative for fear of losing their jobs, admitting to me that those who made errors were punished. But can there be creativity without errors?

The answer brings me to rule number one in removing creativity inhibitors: Leaders should work with employees to reduce fear. In addition, leaders should communicate tolerance of errors during the research stages of a project. Then they must institute a system that communicates errors to others so the errors won't be repeated. Innovation should be rewarded—research errors should not be punished.

Rule number two: Add humor and levity to the workplace. At least, allow soothing music. When the office is too quiet, creativity is stifled.

Relaxing the dress code for those who don't see customers or don't need to be in the office is rule number three. Acceptable, casual, loose clothing allows a better flow of creativity than a tightly buttoned collar, tie, or suit. *Casual* should be well defined in writing so people will comply with a relaxed dress code.

Rule number four: Allow people to decorate their office as long as the decor meets overall company standards.

4. Creative People

It stands to reason that creative people produce more innovations than people who are not creative. If you want to recruit workers to produce innovations, there are certain qualities to search for. Most studies indicate that intelligence does not correlate with creativity.[2] In fact, people with average intelligence can be more creative than people with high intelligence. The secret lies not in the level of intelligence but in the cultivation of creativity. During this discussion, I use talent and skill interchangeably. Creativity is natural but must be cultivated through training and application.

Usually, when you think of creative people, you may think of off-the-wall artists and musicians who have exhibited unusual behaviors—cutting off an ear or living a totally secluded life. These characteristics are exceptions, not the general rule. Most creative people are not eccentric and function well in the workplace. They are crucial to moving the organization forward. People who have developed their creative side can be found in every field, not just in music and art.

Over the past decade, I have observed several qualities most creative people have in common, although some work at developing these qualities more than others. Truly creative people are quite complex and difficult to really know. Just when you think their behavior is predictable, they shift patterns and again become a mystery.

It is this personal complexity that makes creative people exciting to be around. They are never boring and, in fact, are easily bored themselves. For their own protection, they keep their activities varied. Unless the work environment is exciting and diverse, creative people will move to another organization. Because they are difficult to relate to on a consistent basis, creative people may find close relationships arduous. They are more task oriented than people oriented, so they would rather leave a relationship than work at it. It is their attitude that if others cannot accept them the way they are, then the others need to make adjustments. But they assume just the opposite attitude when they are pursuing a goal.

Truly creative people like to set goals and work hard to reach them. Sometimes the path to their goal seems unstructured, especially to organized, rigid personality types. While working on something, creative people may lose all sense of time. They may be late for appointments or ignore the clock to the point that they show up at home three hours beyond the time promised. They have the ability to become immersed in a task and ignore all distractions. This skill of deep concentration causes them to close out the external world. When these creative geniuses are focused on the task at hand, they are pursuing constant improvement—almost to the point of perfectionism. They want their discoveries to work better and better. It is difficult for them to give up on trying to refine their innovation. Sometimes, intervention is necessary to stop the creative person from incessant refining.

Creative individuals dislike interruptions. They like to establish a state of mental flow and stay totally focused on meeting the goal or working on the desired task. They like to govern their own breaks and vacations. They may seem to go off on tangents, but these extra activities have meaning. They will interrupt themselves, but woe to the person who interrupts them.

High energy and youthfulness characterize a creative person. They are fun to be around when they are in a good mood because they are so playful and childlike. It seems as though they are exploring things through the refreshing eyes of a child. Their spontaneity is contagious. They are curious about areas that others would totally overlook. By being observant, they tend to be able to create metaphors easily and transfer ideas from one set of circumstances to another.

Typically, creative individuals find it difficult to settle on a college major; they like everything. Decisions come hard because they feel they have so many positive choices. They are fearful that they will miss out on something interesting and rewarding. While inviting new ideas, they are very open to novel approaches to problem solving.

Self-centeredness can be a performance inhibitor for creative people. They like to work independently and don't always perform well as team players. They have been accused of being too opinionated and not afraid to speak their mind, behavior that can lead to interpersonal conflict. Although open to new ideas, if they have a specific mind-set, it is difficult to convince them of alternatives, and this stubbornness may come across as intolerance. Such persistence is helpful in the discovery stages of innovation, but taken to extremes, it can be a negative trait.

Many knowledge workers fit the description of creative people. They enjoy creative license and expect artistic space. Great leaders understand the importance of encouraging creative people to pursue their areas of interest and provide the resources to allow them to do so.

5. Grasping the Big Picture

A broad-based perspective is necessary for establishing the boundaries of innovation. This could be paradoxical in that innovation involves open-endedness. Then why should boundaries exist? An innovation must be useful to the end user. In a for-profit organization, its success is determined by how it affects the bottom line. In schools, innovation will probably affect student performance. Nonprofit organizations hope that innovations will attract donor funding as well as aid in accomplishing their mission. So, yes, there must be guidelines for creativity to become innovation.

Visioning sessions are helpful in grasping the big picture. I have worked with various organizations—universities, energy companies, state governments, and churches—in such events. In these sessions, it is important to have a facilitator knowledgeable about both the organization and current big-picture issues. The participants engage in developing a collective vision of the organization and all external issues that will affect its future directions. The facilitator guides the group in answering a series of questions. The participants can then name and prioritize initiatives for innovation. All types of organizations can participate in this process, which is not designed solely for business. The following questions should be addressed:

1. In the broadest sense, what business is our organization in?
2. What products and services do we now offer?
3. How is each product and service distributed?
4. What is the customer rating of each product and service?
5. How does each product and service perform in the marketplace?
6. What DynaForces discussed in Chapter 3 affect our organization?
7. How does each DynaForce affect our organization?
8. What are the possible countertrends to the macrotrends in questions 6 and 7 above?
9. How might our present products and services be changed to participate better in the trends or countertrends listed above?
10. How might our organization engage our products and services in e-commerce?
11. What new products and services could we introduce in order to participate in these trends or countertrends?

When considering these questions, have a scribe record the answers for later distribution to team members and for prioritization. Review the DynaForces in Chapter 3 before answering questions 6 and 7. Also take time to consider other general trends that might affect your product or service line. Here are a few:

- Time is a premium to your customer.
- Organizations are going out to the customer more than the customer is coming in to them.
- More women will continue to enter the workforce.
- The Hispanic population will continue to grow in the United States and will increase in buying influence.
- An explosive number of people are using the Internet.
- The desire to purchase everything from banking services to clothes anytime and anywhere is increasing.

In assessing countertrends in question 8, remember that a countertrend is a movement in the opposite direction from the trend.

There may be many opportunities for organizations that catch the wave of a countertrend. An example of a countertrend is tribalism. As the world becomes more diverse and inclusive, people want to be with people who share their same heritage or values—hence the movement to social tribes. Numerous trends running counter to big-picture trends can be addressed.

6. Involving the Whole Person

For creativity to thrive, the whole person must be involved. Figure 10.1 shows that the physical, intellectual, spiritual, and relational parts of the individual must be accessed. Creativity was once considered a soft skill—mostly feminine. Now we recognize that this skill directly affects an organization's bottom line and is a part of the androgynous workplace I have already discussed.

In creativity, a person should be physically involved as much as possible. All five senses can be stimulated. Colors, smells, sounds, tangible objects, even items to stimulate the taste buds help develop ideas.

Ideas spring from the intellect. Although there is no direct correlation between degree of intelligence and creative genius, it stands to reason that creative people need at least average intelligence levels to make discoveries and draw conclusions from observations. A certain degree of wisdom is necessary for creativity to abound. Both mind and soul are involved in generating wisdom. Knowledge and vision produce wisdom. The late Jonas Salk believed that an idea is as important as the human gene for survival of the species.[3]

Passion emanates from the soul. Creativity dissipates without passion. Burning desire, a buy-in with the emotions, motivation, and drive—all are necessary for creativity to be productive. Our technology-driven, high-paced work environments are causing burnout. This state of mind and soul is not conducive to innovation. Organizations cannot sustain themselves if people lose their zest for new discoveries. For instance, Mattel has found that programming weeklong time-outs for courses on topics apart from work issues rejuvenates its Barbie doll designers.[4]

I often hear inventors and entrepreneurs say, "It's not about the money." These resourceful people have the same passion whether their incomes are in the thousands of dollars or the billions. There is excitement in the quest. The journey of discovery is the real reward—not their stock portfolio values.

Most creative people are autonomous; and most teams naturally inhibit autonomy. However, creativity multiplies when incubated through teamwork. The team must be especially designed to foster innovation. The inclination of a team, then, is not to nurture individuality while simultaneously promoting seamless collaboration. For creativity to flourish, innovative personalities must polish their relational skills in order to cooperate with other team members. In assessing creative personality characteristics, remember that a creative individual sometimes makes bold, opinionated comments to other group members. This being the case, all team members should practice communicating with courtesy and respect to augment the flow of ideas.

Stuart Bacon, an advertising and public relations agency, is a consistent winner of regional and national accolades. "At Stuart Bacon, we work to create a good environment, share in our success, offer opportunities for professional development, and find reasons for unbridled, unscheduled joy and rejuvenation," says Jim Stuart, CEO of this Fort Worth, Texas, agency.

"For instance, here are some examples of how we work," he adds. "Every other Friday morning, our account service staff meets with me at Four Star Coffee Bar for 'Java, Jabber, & Jim,' an open discussion of problems or challenges in serving our clients or a review of opportunities we should capitalize on to improve our service to clients."

The agency has also established a 20-minute freestyle, freewheeling brainstorming session for staff members. This lively session, "Short & Sweet Inspiration," gives any employee a chance to contribute a solution to a creative or design challenge or simply to learn more about a client's product or service.

"An exciting, stimulating, creative working environment is an important component of doing a good job for clients as well as enhancing our working lives together," Stuart continues. Stuart and President Randy Bacon motivate and retain employees by these tenets: Everyone contributes to the effort; change is the only option; guard, honor, and exercise traditions; environment is part of the team. "Our innovative process," Stuart concludes, "can be summed up in our purpose statement: We create. We communicate. We inspire."

7. New Thinking

Great leaders comprehend the need to promote new ways of thinking about challenges. Many of the approaches to problem solving are based on conditioning—a certain kind of problem evokes thinking patterns based on past experience. One of the first lessons in Psychology 101 is the study of Pavlov's dogs. After feeding them several times, Pavlov conditioned them to salivate at the sight of food in expectation of being fed. Likewise, humans mentally categorize challenges and automatically respond by trying to resolve the problem just as they have done before.

In promoting new thinking, leaders encourage people to approach each challenge as if they had never experienced anything like it before. And indeed they may not have. Earlier I mentioned the seven kinds of intelligence identified by Harvard University's Dr. Howard Gardner. It is important for people to identify the dominant intelligence they use in problem solving and continue to use it. For example, if you solve problems visually, then draw a picture of the problem plus your solutions and paths of reasoning. If you learn best by doing, then you should actually simulate reality and physically immerse yourself into the problem in order to live the solutions. If problems cannot be created in a lab-type environment, then you might portray a drama in which the problem interacts with you and other characters; or you might trigger your imagination to such a degree that the situation comes to life in your mind. At first, these approaches are uncomfortable in a more sophisticated environment. However, over time, they seem more reasonable.

New thinking also involves honing one's observation skills—even transferring ideas through analyzing metaphors. For example, when organizational development specialists observed that biological systems had much in common with organizational systems, they began to compare organizations with living organisms. Viewing a company or an association as a living organism was a totally new approach unlike the belief that organizations were static and lifeless. With this new approach, dealing with changes became easier because now a model for observation was available.

Keen observation can be compared with a connect-the-dots exercise. A certain degree of knowledge is required to solve a problem in any field. To make observations and connect them in a viable solution requires expertise, imagination, and practicality. I recommend a creative team composed of an expert in the problem area plus people from outside the field of focus. Although a certain degree of knowledge is required, too much specialized knowledge in a field can be detrimental to creativity. Outsiders lend added perspective. Leaders can become too entrenched in habitual thinking, thus making it impossible to see fresh approaches and ideas. Wise leaders recognize this potential problem and summon the right blend of help in establishing new ways of organizational thinking.

Brainstorming sessions are helpful. Total openness to novel ideas without limits should occur at this stage. Feasibility and budget constraints can be considered later. The brainstorming phase is solely for new approaches, some of which may seem strange and off the wall. Of course, in a later stage, these ideas must be balanced with customer response and profit potential. Yet nonprofits must also consider board approval, customer feedback, and budget constrictions.

8. Experiential Training

The best training for creativity is either in a simulated environment or on a real work assignment. Not all innovation is the result of design. Some new discoveries are made in the course of a work assignment either through serendipity or experimentation with new uses for present products or services.

Leaders who are open to providing process choices foster innovation. While mutually defining the problem to be solved and determining parameters for innovation, including rigid deadlines, the group or individuals can then be left to their own ideas. Leaders help with general directions. Workers make choices in the process of discovery. This trust and freedom for trial and error provide priceless on-the-job training. Employees of the 3M Company, which has long had a reputation for innovation, are encouraged to be inventive. An indication that this experiential training works is the many products marketed by 3M that are employee innovations. The major one that comes to mind is Post-it notes.

While allowing experiential training to take place, it is best to ask the workers assigned to a task to align the organization's core competencies with the desired innovation. For example, the global steel industry continues to find new ways to use its product. In staying with its core competency and inventing new uses as well as creating new materials as derivatives of the original product, the industry can continue to thrive. In effect, most every innovation is the result of experiential training. Although the innovation may rely on a textbook process, the actual discovery is new for every innovation.

9. Nurturing Autonomy

Leaders must walk a tightrope in trying to balance individual creativity with group collaboration. Care must be taken not to stifle the contribution that each individual can make. Innovation teams must be designed to nurture the creativity of every team member—not just a few. Leaders can carefully choose each team member so there will be a balance of assertiveness. As I noted earlier, teams tend to adopt the personality and direction of a dominant team member, but this tendency defeats the purpose of innovation.

Autonomy may be nurtured by appointing to the team only one person with a specific set of skills and using only one person from each discipline, such as marketing or engineering. Not all innovations are consummated by teams, for individuals working autonomously continue to be inventive. The two considerations when deciding whether to appoint an individual or a team to work on an innovation project are: (1) the required turnaround time and (2) whether a product or service needs improvement versus a new product or service design.

If the turnaround time is short, it is difficult in many cases to assemble an effective team, but fast-working teams are recommended to work on a new design. The best time to assign an individual to an innovative project is when a product or service needs improvement only and the turnaround time is short. All other combinations lend themselves better to teams that allow member autonomy.

WAYS TO MEASURE INNOVATION

By developing special measurements of innovation, an organization can tabulate progress and assess its relative position in the marketplace. Even the measurement of innovation requires creativity. Many organizations gauge innovation on an annual basis. However, some innovations take several years to develop, a consideration that must be taken into account. Below are 11 ideas for measuring innovation, although the list is not exhaustive, and each organization must use the methods that serve it best:

1. Number of patents, copyrights, trademarks, and service marks filed per year
2. Percent of revenue generated by products less than three years old
3. Percent of sales increase (or decrease) resulting from new products and services
4. Percent of change in stock prices after the introduction of a new product or service
5. Number of new products and services introduced per year
6. Percent of all products and services less than three years old that are now being marketed
7. Percent of before-tax or after-tax profits that a new product or service generates
8. The ratio of before-tax or after-tax profits generated by new products or services to the amount invested in R&D for that new product or service
9. For schools, measurement of the change in test scores after introduction of new teaching methods
10. For churches, measurement of change in attendance after introduction of a new program or type of worship service
11. For governments, measurement of change in process timing or change in constituent complaints after introduction of an innovation

This list of suggestions can certainly be expanded. Each organization must develop its own measurements that best indicate what its leaders need to know. For example, Dr. Michael E. Porter of Harvard University has developed an Innovation Index used by the Council on Competitiveness (www.compete.org, or 202-682-4292) as a comparative tool to rank nations against one another in their degree of innovation.[5] Your organization might develop its own index to rank it against other organizations in your same industry, but such a formulation would require a statistician and is beyond the scope of this discussion.

It is also necessary to define an innovation timetable. Most organizations define *innovation* as a product or service introduced within the last three years. Some organizations go out as far as five years while others go down to as few as six months. After measuring innovation over a specific period, your organization can design an innovation strategy that will allow it to map out how often innovations must be introduced to constantly renew the enterprise.

Only through regular renewal can organizations sustain themselves. Innovation, then, is the ticket to organizational sustainability.

AN URGENT CALL TO ACTION

We have reached the point in the course of human events where leaders must choose boldly either to lead, follow, or step aside. I urge you to opt for greatness. Those leaders of significance will be courageous enough to take action. The human character is reflected in what the person does. It is not enough to *be*. Great leaders must *do*.

On the road to greatness, leaders will succeed by having the courage to publicly fail, achieve excellence by daring to confront their own mediocrity, and squarely face the future by fearlessly letting go of the past.

We have explored in detail the five steps for moving from being a *good* leader to becoming a *great* leader: Orchestrate a 360° worldview, order the chaos, blend multiple organizational models, engage the whole person, and ignite innovation.

These five initiatives require investment of your time, energy, and self-introspection. I urge you to execute boldly, step forward courageously, and lead responsibly as if your organization's prosperity depends on it—because it does.

Godspeed, great leader.

 LEADERSHIP STRATEGIES

✓ Survey your organizational surroundings and note any part of the environment that may be inhibiting creativity.

✓ Design a plan for countering each creativity inhibitor.

✓ Hire a consultant who specializes in creativity and innovation to conduct a makeover of your present spatial environment—including color schemes, furniture, sounds, and use of natural light and plants.

✓ If your organization has telecommuters or other types of virtual relationships, implement a strategy whereby each worker receives support in setting up a creative working environment.

✓ Implement creative sessions in such unique places as organizational retreat rooms, coffeehouses, and amusement parks. Only your imagination can limit you.

✓ Set up a system for introducing innovations and measuring their effectiveness This system will include goals for frequency of introducing innovations and the percentage of the innovation's bottom-line contribution.

✓ Determine how your organization can innovate by using the Internet. If your enterprise is already using an Internet Web site and/or is engaged in e-commerce, measure current success and implement creative improvements.

QUESTIONS FOR CONTEMPLATION

1. On a scale of 1 to 5, with 1 being the lowest, rate your organization's ability to be innovative.

2. On that same 1 to 5 scale, rate your organization on these nine ingredients of innovation: (1) adequate budget for innovative activities; (2) physical environment that promotes creativity; (3) elimination of creativity inhibitors; (4) recruiting creative people; (5) grasping the big picture for nurturing innovation; (6) involving the whole person; (7) promoting new thinking; (8) training experientially; and (9) nurturing autonomy.

3. If you rated any of the areas in number 2 below 3, what are some actions that can be taken to elevate that score?

ENDNOTES

1. As reported by the Council on Competitiveness, *Challenges* 12, no. 1 (Winter 1999): 6.

2. Michael Michalko, "Thinking Like a Genius: Eight Strategies Used by the Super-creative from Aristotle and Leonardo to Einstein and Edison," *The Futurist* (May 1998): 21–25.

3. As reported in Carolyn Corbin, *Strategies 2000* (Austin, Texas: Eakin Press, 1986 and 1989), 30.

4. Jerd Smith, "The Spirit of Business: Boulder Institute Tries to Connect Values of Corporations to the People They Employ," *Denver Rocky Mountain News*, 9 May 1999, 1G. Reprinted with permission of the *Denver Rocky Mountain News*.

5. Council on Competitiveness, *Challenges* 12, no. 1 (Winter 1999): 1.

BIBLIOGRAPHY

Alford, Randall J. "Going Virtual, Getting Real." *Training & Development* (January 1999): 34–44.

Alzheimer's Association. "Alzheimer's Disease Costs Businesses Billions." *Advances* 18, no. 4 (Winter 1999): 1.

Amabile, Teresa M. "How to Kill Creativity." *Harvard Business Review* (September-October 1998): 77–87.

Anders, George. "The View from the Top." *Wall Street Journal*, 12 July 1999, 4E.

Anfuso, Dawn. "Core Values Shape W.L. Gore's Innovative Culture." *Workforce* (March 1999): 48–53.

Apgar, Mahlon, IV. "The Alternative Workplace: Changing Where and How People Work." *Harvard Business Review* (May-June 1998): 121–36.

Arthur, Jodi Spiegel. "Growing Up." *Human Resource Executive* (18 May 1999): 30–34.

Augustine, Norman R. "Reshaping an Industry: Lockheed Martin's Survival Story." *Harvard Business Review* (May-June 1997).

Bartlett, Christopher A., and Sumantra Ghoshal. "Changing the Role of Top Management: Beyond Systems to People." *Harvard Business Review* (May-June 1995): 132–42.

Bernstein, Aaron. "We Want You to Stay. Really." *Business Week*, 22 June 1998, 67–72.

Blum, Milton L., and James C. Naylor. *Industrial Psychology: Its Theoretical and Social Foundations.* New York: Harper and Row, 1968.

Briggs, John C. "The Promise of Virtual Reality." *The Futurist* (September-October 1996): 13–18.

Brokaw, Tom. *The Greatest Generation.* New York: Random House, 1998.

Bruzzese, Anita. "Young and Restless." *Human Resource Executive* (July 1999): 66–68.

Camina, Catalina. "Spirituality on the Hill." *Dallas Morning News*, 17 February 1996: 1G.

Carey, Rita. "Work in the 21st Century: A Series of Trapezes?" *Futures Research Quarterly* (Fall 1997): 31–38.

Caudron, Shari. "Create an Empowering Environment." *Personnel Journal* (September 1995): 28–36.

Charan, Ram, and Geoffrey Colvin. "Why CEOs Fail." *Fortune*, 21 June 1999, 68–78.

Clark, Kathryn F. "Diamonds in the Rough." *Human Resource Executive* (18 June 1999).

Corbin, Carolyn. *Conquering Corporate Codependence*. Englewood Cliffs, New Jersey: Prentice-Hall, 1993.

——. *Strategies 2000*. Austin, Texas: Eakin Press, 1986, 1990.

Costello, Bill. "Make Money by Thinking the Unthinkable." *The Futurist* (May 1999): 30–34.

de Llosa, Patty. "Why Companies Fail." *Fortune*, 14 November 1994, 52–68.

Dolainski, Stephen. "Partnering with the (School) Board." *Workforce* (May 1997): 28–37.

Dorsey, David. "The New Spirit of Work." *Fast Company*, August 1998, 125–34.

Drucker, Peter F. "The Age of Social Transformation." *Quality Digest* (February 1995).

——. "The Discipline of Innovation." *Harvard Business Review* (November-December 1998): 149–57.

——. "Management's New Paradigms." *Forbes*, 5 October 1998, 156.

Drucker Peter F. et al. "Looking Ahead: Implications of the Present." *Harvard Business Review* (September-October 1997).

Dumaine, Brian. "Payoff from the New Management." *Fortune*, 13 December 1993, 103–10.

Estrada, Anette W., and Sander S. Wechsler. "Are You Euro-Fluent?" *Journal of Accountancy* (June 1999): 22–24, 26–27.

Flynn, Gillian. "Diversity Programs." *Workforce* (December 1998): 27–32.

Folpe, Jane M., and Maroney Tyler. "The Hottest Job in the Old Economy." *Fortune*, 24 May 1999, 108–10.

Freeman, Richard B. "Toward an Apartheid Economy." *Harvard Business Review* (September-October 1996).

Fulmer, Robert M., and Stacey Wagner. "Leadership Lessons from the Best." *Training & Development* (March 1999): 29–32.

Galagan, Patricia A. "Peter Drucker." *Training & Development* (September 1998): 23–24.

Gardener, Howard. *Frames of the Mind*. Reprint, New York: Basic Books, 1993.

Garten, Jeffrey E. "Can the World Survive the Triumph of Capitalism?" Book Review, *Harvard Business Review* (January-February 1997).

Gates, Bill. *The Road Ahead*. New York: Viking, 1995.

Goleman, Daniel. *Emotional Intelligence*. New York: Bantam Books, 1995.

———. *Working with Emotional Intelligence*. New York: Bantam Books, 1998.

Granberry, Michael. "Jeff Bezos." *The Dallas Morning News*, 8 August 1999, 4E.

Griffith, Carolyn. "Building a Resilient Workforce." *Training* (January 1998): 54–60.

Hadnot, Ira J. "Digital Divide." *The Dallas Morning News*, 27 July 1999, 10J.

Hall, Cheryl. "A Gen-X State of Mind." *The Dallas Morning News*, 25 July 1999, 1A.

Harvard Business Review Editors. "Looking Ahead: Implications of the Present." *Harvard Business Review* (September-October 1997): 18–32.

Hill, Linda, and Suzy Wetlaufer. "Leadership When There Is No One to Ask: An Interview with ENI's Franco Bernabe." *Harvard Business Review* (July-August 1998): 81–94.

Hoff, Robert D. with Ellen Neuborne and Heather Green. "Amazon. com: The Wild World of E.Commerce." *Business Week,* 14 December 1998, 106-19.

Huang, Thomas, and Manuel Mandoza. "The Importance of Being Earnest." *The Dallas Morning News,* 7 March 1999. 6F.

Jones, Gregg. "Battered Economies in Asia Teetering on Edge of Recovery." *The Dallas Morning News,* 1 August 1999. 35A.

Jossi, Frank. "Solid Foundations." *Human Resource Executive* (19 October 1998): 49-51.

Kahaner, Larry. *Competitive Intelligence.* New York: Simon & Schuster, 1996.

Kruger, Pamela. "A Leader's Journey." *Fast Company,* June 1999.

Kunde, Diana. "Leaping into Leadership." *The Dallas Morning News,* 16 June 1999, 1A.

Kurzweil, Ray. *The Age of Spiritual Machines: When Computers Exceed Human Intelligence.* New York: Viking, 1999.

Laabs, Jennifer J. "Balancing Spirituality and Work." *Personnel Journal* (September 1995).

———. "Downshifters." *Personnel Journal* (March 1996): 62-76.

———. "Has Downsizing Missed Its Mark?" *Workforce* (April 1999): 30-38.

———. "The New Loyalty: Grasp It. Earn It. Keep It." *Workforce* (November 1998): 34-39.

———. "Pick the Right People." *Workforce* (November 1998): 50-56.

———. "Satisfy Them with More Than Money." *Workforce* (November 1998): 40-43.

———. "Show Them Where You're Headed." *Workforce* (November 1998): 45-48.

Labich, Kenneth. "Fasten Your Seat Belts." *Fortune,* 10 May 1999, 114-18.

Landers, Jim. "Business Must Do More to Help Educate Workers: Key to Global Competitiveness Lies in Training." *The Dallas Morning News,* 11 March 1996, 1A.

Lauerman, Connie. "Transform Your Work through Spirituality, Author Urges." *The Dallas Morning News*, 5 April 1999, 2D.

Levinson, Marc. "Capitalism with a Safety Net?" *Harvard Business Review* (September-October 1996).

Linkow, Peter. "What Gifted Strategic Thinkers Do." *Training & Development* (July 1999): 34–37.

Malone, Thomas W., and Robert J. Laubacher. "The Dawn of the E-Lance Economy." *Harvard Business Review* (September-October 1998): 145–52.

McGinn, Daniel, and John McCormick. "Your Next Job." *Newsweek*, 1 February 1999, 43–45.

McGrath, Rita Gunther, and Ian C. MacMillan. "Discovery-Driven Planning." *Harvard Business Review* (July-August 1995): 44–54.

McRae, Hamish. *The World in 2020.* Boston: Harvard Business School Press, 1994.

Meister, Jeanne C. "Extending the Short Shelf Life of Knowledge." *Training & Development* (June 1998): 52–59.

Michalko, Michael. "Thinking Like a Genius: Eight Strategies Used by the Supercreative from Aristotle and Leonardo to Einstein and Edison." *The Futurist* (May 1998).

Michener, James A. *This Noble Land, My Vision for America.* New York: Random House, 1996.

Mitchell, Russ. "How to Manage Geeks." *Fast Company*, June 1999, 174–80.

Morris, Betsy. "Addicted to Sex." *Fortune*, 10 May 1999, 66–80.

Munk, Nina. "Finished at Forty." *Fortune*, 1 February 1999, 50–66.

Nelson, Jack. "More Spies Targeting U.S. Firms." *The Dallas Morning News*, 12 January 1998, 4D.

Nollen, Stanley, and Helen Axel. *Managing Contingent Workers: How to Reap the Benefits and Reduce the Risks.* New York: Amacom, 1996.

Pagell, Ruth. "Economic Espionage." August/September 1998, 23–30. <www.online.com/database>

———. "Economic Espionage and Strategic Intelligence." *The Journal of AGSI* (March 1999): 36–41.

Porter, Michael E. "Clusters and the New Economics of Competition." *Harvard Business Review* (November-December 1998): 77–90.

Poussaint, Alvin F., M.D. *Single Parenthood: Implications for American Society.* University of Texas at Austin, Texas: Hogg Foundation for Mental Health, 1997.

Quinn, James Brian, Philip Anderson, and Sydney Finkelstein. "Managing Professional Intellect: Making the Most of the Best." *Harvard Business Review* (March-April 1996): 71–80.

Rappaport, Alfred. "New Thinking on How to Link Executive Pay with Performance." *Harvard Business Review* (March-April 1999): 91–101.

———. Religion in the Workplace Mini-Survey, Society for Human Resource Management (SHRM) Issues Management Program, Society for Human Resource Management, January 1977.

Rhinesmith, Stephen H. "My Days with Peter Drucker." *Training & Development* (September 1998): 24–25.

Rifkin, Jeremy. *The End of Work: The Decline of the Global Labor Force and the Dawn of the Post-Market Era.* New York: A Jeremy P. Tarcher/Putnam Book published by G. P. Putnam's Sons, 1995.

Robertson, James. *Beyond the Dependency Culture: People, Power, and Responsibility.* Westport, Conn.: PRAEGER, 1998.

Robinson, Alan G., and Sam Stern. *Corporate Creativity: How Innovation and Improvement Actually Happen.* San Francisco: Berrett-Koehler Publishers, 1997.

Rossett, Allison. "Knowledge Management Meets Analysis." *Training & Development* (May 1999): 63–68.

Salopek, Jennifer J. "Train Your Brain." *Training & Development* (October 1998): 27–33.

Schlender, Brent. "E-Business According to Gates." *Fortune,* 12 April 1999, 72–79.

Schwartz, Nelson D. "The Tech Boom Will Keep on Rocking." *Fortune,* 15 February 1999, 65–80.

Schwartz, Peter. *The Art of the Long View.* New York: Doubleday Currency, 1991.

Solomon, Charlene Marmer. "Brace for Change." *Global Workforce* (January 1999).

——. "Keep Them!" *Workforce* (August 1997): 46–52.

Smith, Jerd. "The Spirit of Business Boulder Instate Tries to Connect Values of Corporations to the People They Employ." *Denver Rocky Mountain News,* 9 May 1999, 1G.

Taylor, William C. "The Leader of the Future." *Fast Company,* June 1999, 130–38.

Thurow, Lester C. *The Future of Capitalism.* New York: William Morrow, 1996.

Toffler, Alvin. *Powershift.* New York: Bantam Books, 1990.

Uchida, Donna with Marvin Cetron and Floretta McKenzie. *Preparing Students for the 21st Century.* Arlington, Virginia: American Association of School Administrators, 1996.

Van Buren, Mark E. "A Yardstick for Knowledge Management." *Training & Development* (May 1999): 71–78.

Waterman, Robert H. Jr., Judith A. Waterman, and Betsy A. Collard. "Toward a Career-Resilient Workforce." *Harvard Business Review* (July-August 1994): 87–95.

Webber, Alan M. "Learning for a Change." *Fast Company,* May 1999, 178–88.

Weiss, Kenneth R. "Generation Why?" *The Dallas Morning News,* 12 January 1998, 1A.

Wolman, William, and Anne Colamosca. *The Judas Economy: The Triumph of Capital and the Betrayal of Work.* Reading, Mass.: Addison-Wesley, 1997.

INDEX

TO CONTACT CAROLYN CORBIN

Carolyn Corbin can be reached for keynote speeches, consulting assignments, and seminars through:

Center for the 21st Century
21 Country Ridge Road
Melissa, TX 75454-8900
972-484-2985 (Dallas area) or 800-788-3199
Fax: 972-838-4355
e-mail: <carolyncorbin@c21c.com>
Web site: <www.c21c.com>

The Center for the 21st Century is a think tank that specializes in innovative business, nonprofit, education, government, religious, and community-based performance interventions. Carolyn Corbin, founder and president, is an internationally renowned consultant, author, speaker, and business futurist.

This consortium of high-level, award-winning, international business experts, social thinkers, and futurists designs programs and interventions in 21st century critical organizational issues. Their expertise lies in the following areas: 360° worldview (big picture) analysis, visioning, leadership in the 21st century e-commerce world, change/chaos management, self-governance, developing the whole person, managing knowledge workers, and special topics researched and developed on request.